Involved with a Cad
for 7 Years
in the Twilight Zone

DARLENE NOLIN

PAGE PUBLISHING, INC.
Conneaut Lake, PA

First originally published by Page Publishing 2020

The information contained in this book is provided for educational purposes only. It is not intended to be taken as legal advice. It is highly recommended the reader consult with a lawyer familiar with US immigration laws for any legal questions he or she may have about their specific legal situation.

The author wrote this book with the intent to share her personal experience in hopes it helps others. The book is a truthful recollection of actual events in the author's life. The names and certain details of the author's life have been changed to maintain anonymity and privacy of the individuals named in the book. Some of the events described in the book have been compressed and some dialogue has been recreated by the author.

This book contains content related to physical and/or mental health issues that the author experienced and/or observed during her journey. The author's comments or opinions related to physical and/or mental health issues she observed should not be considered a medical opinion. No licensed medical practitioner has reviewed these opinions made by the author.

ISBN 978-1-64701-143-7 (pbk)
ISBN 978-1-64701-144-4 (digital)

Printed in the United States of America

I would like to thank my mother, for all her love and support before, during, and after the twilight zone years.

In loving memory of my late father, Daniel L. Nolin.

To my daughter Alyssa who lights up a room with her smile and fills it with contagious laughter.

To my son, Richard, who amazes me with his intuitive mind.

To my daughter Rachel who inspires me with her courage.

To my grandchildren Angel, Noah, Zoey, Braeden and Brody—all of my love.

Contents

Acknowledgements

If it wasn't for the encouragement of my Literary Development Agent this book never would have seen the light of day. Thank you, Robert for giving me the platform to tell my story.

Thank you to everyone at Southern New Hampshire University for giving me the support and the skills that I needed to make this book a reality.

To everyone who gave me their love and support along the way, I am blessed to have you all in my life.

Introduction

No Green Card=No Matrimony

No Green Card=No Matrimony is a guide for the smart, independent American woman who wants to believe her partner has the right motives for marriage but can't seem to shake the warning signs that his intentions are disingenuous. Often witty and always truthful, the author speaks to those of us who have had relationships with foreign men and some of the pitfalls that can accompany it. Unfortunately, many intelligent women ignore red flags because they have waited until after they've fallen in love to start asking important questions. How can you tell if your man truly loves you or is only in it for the citizenship?

How can you listen to both your heart and head? How can you give love and protect yourself and your interest? Let this handy checklist be your compass. Learn what you truly value in a relationship and have a few laughs along the way (J. King, 2015).

Woman's Justice Publications (WJP) has heard the cries of several women who became victims of marriage fraud and who have not been properly defended by the current US Immigration Law. (WJP) believes in writing books that are candid and that will help women make better decisions so that they don't end up victims of inadequate legal protection.

Author: David Seminara, consular officer in Skopje, Macedonia, and Budapest, Hungary.

Key Points:

- Marriage to an American citizen remains the most common path to US residency and/or citizenship for foreign nationals with more than 2.3 million foreign nationals gaining lawful permanent resident (LPR) status in this manner between 1998 and 2007.

- More than 25 percent of all green cards issued in 2007 were to the spouses of American citizens. In 2006 and 2007, there were nearly twice as many green cards issued to the spouses of American citizens than were issued for all employment-based immigration categories combined. The number of foreign nationals obtaining green cards based on marriage to an American has more than doubled since 1985 and has quintupled since 1970.

- Despite these statistics, marriage fraud for immigration gets very little notice or debate in the public arena and the State Department and Department of Homeland Security have nowhere near the resources needed to combat the problem. Attention to fraud is not just for the integrity of the legal immigration system but also for security reasons. If small-time con artists and third-world gold diggers can obtain green cards with so little resistance, then surely terrorists can do (and have done) the same.

- An overwhelming percentage of all petitions to bring foreign spouses or fiancés to the United States illegally (or to help them adjust visa status if they are already in the United States on nonimmigrant visas) are approved—even in cases where the couple may only have met over the internet and may not even share a common language.

- Marriage to an American is the clearest pathway to citizenship for an illegal alien. A substantial number of illegal aliens ordered removed (many of whom have criminal records) later resurface as marriage-based green card applicants. Waivers granted to those marrying US citizens can eliminate ineligibilities for green cards, including the three- to ten-year bar on entry for those with long periods of illegal presence.

- The decision-making authority for green card applications lies with USCIS officials who rely almost exclusively on documents, records, and photographs with little opportunity for interviews or investigations. Consular officers reviewing cases overseas do live interviews and can initiate local investigations but may only approve petitions, not deny them (D. Crocetti, 2007).

Don Crocetti noted age difference to be a significant factor in foreign national marriage fraud. Attorney representation also was an indicator for fraud.

He had never held a job—common for male immigrant visa applicants from Macedonia and Kosovo.

US immigration lists one of the types of marriage fraud as being "A foreign national defrauds a US citizen who believes the marriage is legitimate."

Senate Holds a Rare Hearing on Immigration-Related Marriage Fraud

The US Senate Judiciary Committee held a rare hearing earlier this month on a long-neglected subject, immigration-related marriage fraud.

Two US citizens came forward to testify that they had been hoodwinked by aliens who subsequently abused the witnesses after securing what they had wanted in the first place—not love and marriage but a green card.

Both of the aliens used K-1 visas to gain admission to the United States, one of the techniques used in this kind of fraud. Citizens ask that the government issue K-1s to their prospective alien spouses; the process assumes that the alien and the citizen will marry within three months of the alien's arrival in the United States and that both citizen and aliens are, in fact, single and eligible for marriage.

The two citizens, apparently brushing aside concerns about their own privacy, were Elena Lopez and Dr. Jamal Hussain; both told how aliens, pretending to love them, had abandoned them once legal status had been obtained. In the case of Lopez, she said that her husband had attempted to strangle her and had aimed a rifle at her, firing blanks and laughing. Hussain's fiancée had apparently been married and divorced earlier, and had not reported those events, as she should have on her visa application. Both citizens suffered financial and emotional losses as a result of this misfiring of the immigration law.

Lopez had a spouse from Holland; Hussain's fiancée was from his native Pakistan. There was a marriage in the first case but none in the second. It was not clear from the testimony, but neither alien apparently has been penalized for this behavior, and both aliens seemed to preserve their legal status.

Both Lopez and Hussain said that their attempts to secure justice from immigration officials were ignored, an important point that, sadly, was not mentioned again in the hearings. We at the Center hear, all too often, how DHS officials ignore evidence presented by citizen victims of marriage fraud; one reason for this is the way that the Violence Against Women Act is written.

In a sense, the hearing had the feel of ships passing in the night. The two victims told how much they had been hurt by official neglect of their complaints. The five government witnesses talked about various processes used to prevent marriage fraud and (as far as I could hear) never mentioned what should be done to help the victims of immigration-related marriage fraud.

The eighth witness was an immigration lawyer, Grace Huang, who warned against causing harm by overreacting to the cited problems and spoke of some occasions when K-1 visas were misused by citizens to exploit alien women. The senators were largely concerned with loopholes in the process and called for more vigilance in the administration of the law. None of these passing ships seemed to communicate with each other.

Sen. Ted Cruz (R-Texas), in a cameo appearance toward the ending of the hearing, substituted for the chairman, Chuck Grassley (R-Iowa), and recalled that the K-1 visa had played a role in the terrorist shooting in San Bernardino.

I hope that this hearing will be as productive as one I attended long ago. That one, on July 26, 1985, was conducted by then-Sen. Alan Simpson (R-Wyo.) and led to the passage of legislation that made it impossible for quick remarriages of fraudsters, establishing a two-year waiting period before the alien/citizen marriage could lead to a green card. This was an important step in the right direction. I was an expert (not a victim) witness at that hearing; most of the other witnesses were citizens telling stories very much like those of Lopez and Hussain. In other words, this is not a new problem (D. North, 2017).

Family Visa Petition

When you hear about US immigration in the news, you most likely will only hear about mass migration at our southern border, illegal immigration, and deportation. How often do you hear about work visas, tourist visas, K-1 fiancé visas, and family visas? There are US citizens at home and abroad that have been affected by current immigration laws that pertain to family visas and K-1 fiancé visas.

Immigration Form I-864, Affidavit of Support, is a vital document you should read before you ever say I do to a foreign national—at home or abroad. If you don't, you may find that you have entered into a legally binding contract with the federal government that will take a huge toll on your financial and emotional well-being should your marriage go south due to no fault of your own.

The immigration Form I-864, Affidavit of Support, is a vital document according to USCIS because it proves that the American citizen who filed a petition for a family visa on behalf of their immigrant spouse meets the financial requirements to support them in the United States and that the foreign national will not become a government charge.

In other words, they won't have to apply for any type of government assistance.

In my case, it was this form that had a big impact on my former immigrant spouse's visa application and, ultimately, my relationship. It was because I did not meet the financial requirements of that form that my spouse's visa application was denied. I was told that I needed to find someone to cosponsor his application.

No one I knew wanted to cosponsor my foreign national spouse's visa application because they never met him in person. All my friends and family could call his bullshit from across the pond. They didn't believe that his intentions for me were genuine. Most of that came from him harassing them over the phone and on the internet. They told me that he was a stark raving mad lunatic with a nefarious agenda.

They believed that he had an ulterior motive, and they were right. I believe he picked me as an easy target. I must have had high levels of empathy.

Not every American/foreign national relationship works or is genuine. It is too high of a gamble to take. Think they love you? They don't. They only want to get the hell out of Dodge and get their hands on that green card, so don't kid yourself. The telltale red flag signs are poverty and desperation to get out of it. Being overboard controlling is not a good sign either.

I wrote this book to share my personal story to help others so they can prevent a similar event from happening in their lives. Hopefully, to see it coming from all the warning signs and stop it before it even takes place.

To be fair though, I have met some American citizens who have married a foreign national immigrant, and their marriages were genuine. I know, and I can say with a hundred percent certainty that I would not take that gamble again.

I will refer to my foreign national ex-spouse as Victor, as in the naked statue of Victor that holds a falcon in his left hand and a sword with his right hand. The statue of Victor can be found in Kalemegdan Fortress, which overlooks the Sava and Danube rivers.

Victor in the beginning of our relationship seemed to be a decent guy; however, as you will notice, his niceness takes on a very nefarious direction as the years go by.

CHAPTER 1

Friend Request

Once upon a time, I was just going about my business as a single parent going through the divorce process. It was around March 2010, almost a year after my dad and paternal grandmother passed away within the space of three weeks of each other. To say that I was vulnerable would have been an understatement.

After my teenage daughter went to school and I had breakfast and coffee, I would go on Facebook to see friends and how they were doing on any given day. We would make plans for the upcoming weekend.

One day, I discovered that I had a friend request, a very odd one at that. His photo did not match his profile. He was about twelve years my junior, and he claimed to be from Beverly Hill, California. I sent him a message and said to him, "You do not look like you are from California!" He appeared to me to look more like a foreign national than an American. I told him that he looked more Greek than anything.

He said, "Close. I am from Macedonia [Northern Greece]."

He was young and handsome. I guess that's what got my attention. You know the old saying "If it looks too good to be true, it is." Well, he was! I asked him why he used a fake American location instead of where he was really from. He said that Facebook would not let him put in his real location. That would be another long string of lies he would weave for the next seven years. It would later prove to be his modus operandi.

Blinded by his charms, I accepted his friend request. At the time, it was all new and exciting. Everyone told me to get rid of him because he was up to no good, but I didn't listen. He told me that they were just jealous because he was young and good-looking. When his obvious signs of deception were pointed out to me, I still could not see the forest for the trees.

Victor would write things on my Facebook page, such as my name with his last name. He would also refer to me as his wife. He sent me glittery graphics with hearts. He went overboard pouring on the charm. He was love bombing me, except at the time I didn't know what that was.

Friends and family members told me that I was being brainwashed by him. I lost a lot of friends back then because of him, and it put a huge strain on family relations as well. Once he got on my Facebook page, he said things to people behind my back. He even sent my own mother an e-mail with some not so nice accusations in it about her, which were not true. Victor never met my mother in person. He fought with a couple of my closest friends online, and they told me to get rid of him. Some tried to point out that he was destroying all my relationships so he could isolate me.

CHAPTER 2

The Kaa and Mowgli Days

Our relationship started out on Facebook but quickly progressed to Skype. He needed an online translator to talk to me. We did not share a common language. That is a *red flag*.

I refer to this as the Kaa and Mowgli days because I was the little jungle boy, and Victor was the hypnotic snake up in the tree that had me in his trance. Oddly enough, *The Jungle Book* Disney cartoon version, not J. R. Kipling's 1894/1967 version, is what I am referring to. It was one of my favorites as a child, ironic as that sounds.

There was a little bit more to this hypnotic state that I did not but should have realized at the time. It was called personal magnetism, and, it had something to do with his eyes. He was les yeux sans visage, eyes without a face, just like the Billy Idol song.

A friend of mine at the time tried to point out to me that he cast some type of love spell. I refused to believe this even though I knew it was possible. Between love spell and brainwashed as people said I was, I started to believe that I might be an unlovable human being. I did, however, relish in the attention he had to give.

Did Victor have me under his spell? Yes, I believe looking back that he did. He was highly skilled in the art of manipulation.

The online relationship progressed into one that I would classify as extremely controlling, Victor wanted me to see him first thing when I woke up and sit there with him all day. Whenever I needed to leave the house, he insisted on waiting there on Skype for me. That should have been another *red flag*. He didn't work!

One day, I suggested that Victor give me his phone number so I could call him. When I got him on the phone, he became very nervous because he could not speak good English. He was afraid that I would make fun of him.

At least I got a better opportunity to hear what Victor's voice sounded like. The phone call was very brief but telling nonetheless. Was I out of my mind? How could I have a long-distance relationship with someone who lived on the other side of the world who could not speak my own language? So much for communication being a vital part of a relationship. I thought maybe it was the international language of love and all the wishy-washy stuff that went along with it. We carried on with this online relationship for about three to four weeks, then he asked if he could come and live with me. Moving a new relationship too fast is also a *red flag*. I was surprised when Victor asked me if I could get him a job where I worked. I told him that I was not currently working at the time. Reluctantly, I said, "Sure. Come on over."

He said, "I can't without a US visa." He then asked if I could find out how I could get him one—another *red flag*.

I began to do some research and then made a few phone calls to no avail. I went to an immigration office close to where I lived, and they told me that he could apply for a tourist visa. When I told Victor this, he suggested that I go get a passport and come to his country. At the time, it seemed a bit impossible since I was a single parent of a teenager and going through a divorce. Victor said he wanted to see if we could have a relationship. I was hesitant since he lived so far away, and I had to find someone to keep an eye on my defiant teen. I could sense some anxiety coming from him, especially when he stood up and walked backward away from his computer and took off all his clothes. Wow! Have you ever seen that picture of the cat with huge eyes? Well, that was me!

While I was applying for my passport, we had an intimate relationship online. *I'll be going to hell in a handbasket for this*, I thought, nonetheless, it was exciting. Looking back on that, I do have regrets.

Yeah, he was smoking hot. Any woman with a pulse would have jumped on that! He knew it, and I knew it. I figured, what the hell, it might as well be me. I deserved it after being cockblocked by my teenage daughter while going through a separation, divorce, and trying to date.

While I was waiting for my passport to arrive, I made plans for my teenager to have someone with her while I took a much-needed vacation. I started to plan my first trip abroad. I considered it to be a four-week vacation and planned it accordingly.

CHAPTER 3

The Blossoming

When my passport arrived, my travel plans were ready. I took a bus to the airport, checked my bags, and waited for two hours to board my first international flight. It was my second time flying. The first time was twenty-two years ago, so I was a bit anxious.

What a long eighteen-hour flight! While flying over the Atlantic Ocean, I asked the flight attendant why the ocean could not be seen out my window. She said, "If we flew below the clouds, the ocean would probably suck us in." For six hours, we flew above the clouds.

When the plane reached Europe, the Irish countryside just before dawn was magical. The streetlights in London just before the sun came up were all in different colors like a rainbow.

I had a four-hour stopover in London at Heathrow Airport. This is not a fun airport to navigate, but nevertheless, I managed. When you cross the Atlantic, you enter a new time zone. When I boarded my next plane to the capital of his country, I noticed it was not as nice as the first plane. This flight took about four hours; however, once again, there was an hour difference in time due to time zone change. Flying from my country to his seemed to feel like I was going back in time. The Carpathian mountain region of Romania gave off an ominous vibe from my plane window. When I arrived sometime in the afternoon at the airport in his country, I noticed that this airport was Third World. I collected my suitcase from baggage and proceeded out the door. I felt as though I was going into the unknown.

There he was. Wow! Much taller in person and strikingly handsome and a big smile on his face. No hug though. He took my bags and led me to his friend's waiting car. Since this friend played a pivotal role in this true story, I will call him Ivan.

All the way from the airport to his home, Victor and I could not keep our hands off each other. When I did manage to come up for a breather, I thought some parts of the capital of his country were beautiful and some Third World. The architecture in this European country was extravagant in some locations. We drove by a section of the city that had two buildings that appeared to have huge bomb holes in them. I was told not to take any pictures of them. It was forbidden.

The next town over was more Third World than the capital. We drove through there and toward where Victor lived.

I can only describe Victor's hometown as Kansas with a European twist. We drove by miles of cornfields, sunflowers, and bee boxes. When we pulled up at his home, I was taken a few steps back. It was run down and very poverty-stricken—another *red flag*.

I got out of the car slowly. I walked toward to front metal gate entrance to the home and waited on the sidewalk for Victor to open the gate. I walked through the gate slowly. On my right, there was a pear tree, clothesline, and a well. In front of me, there was what appeared to be a massive garden with many fruit trees beyond a wire fence. To the left, I saw a mound of dirt with trash and rubble from the side of the building. I looked up to see a pigeon sitting where there used to be a window of the upper floor of the building that would appear to be the attic or second floor. The overall first impression I got of this place was that it had been run down and neglected for decades due to poverty.

Victor introduced me to his family, who all ran out of the house when they heard us pull up and were now standing outside in front of me, smiling. His mother, with her gray hair in a bun, seemed like a very nice lady. I would later dub her to be Norman Bates's mother from the movie *Psycho*. His sister-in-law was a tiny woman of about 4'11" and a hundred pounds soaking wet. Victor's niece and two nephews were adorable. I picked the two youngest kids up and gave them a hug. I would meet his brother later that day because he was at work. Victor would later tell me that his brother worked for American Steel.

When I entered the building, I noticed that the front brick stairs were in need of serious repair.

Inside the door to my left were two doors with stained glass windows. To my right, there was a barn-style double sink and a back door that was not made to keep out extreme cold temperatures. Straight ahead, there was what looked to be a bedroom. Victor and I went into the first door on the left, which was his room to chill for a while.

Although I was extremely exhausted, I was too excited to take a jet lag nap. I just sat there and stared at him like wow, just wow!

Victor told me he would make us some dinner. He left the room and came back with some fish. When he put the plate of fish in front of me, I was a bit hesitant to eat them because the heads and tails were still on them. They were partially frozen smelts battered in flour and fried in sunflower oil. My dinner was literally looking at me. He broke me half a loaf of bread. Not wanting to offend him, I began to eat. As we ate, I would put one fish at a time from my plate into his, so I had to eat less. He finally noticed when the more he ate, the more he had left. He finally said, "Please stop!"

I did. It was a memorable dinner though nevertheless.

I asked him where the bathroom was. He told me to walk out into the other room and go out the back door and walk down the path. While walking down the path, I noticed I was walking past a pile of garbage. When I got down to the end of the path, I found a tin overhang with a hole in the ground and a million flies. I would later dub this as the *shit* shack. I convinced myself that there was no way I was going to be able to go there. I walked back up the path and back into the house where his sister-in-law looked at me with a look of pity. I walked back into his room and told him that there was no way I was going to use this arrangement. He asked why, and I told him I could not stand in the human waste of others and hover over a million flies buzzing all over my ass. He thought my analogy was funny. I did not. His solution to this was to get me a bucket and put it in his room.

The next day, Victor showed me around his home. I saw baby chicks and ducklings. The garden there was like no other garden I've ever seen. It had plum trees, cherry trees, raspberry bushes, and an apple tree. The size of the garden was massive. I would estimate that it was about a hundred feet long and fifty feet wide with a three-foot island of grass right down the middle of it. We took pictures of it. It was a beautiful spring day in May, and the whole place was blossoming.

One day, Victor told me that there was a festival coming to his village called the festival of the dead. *Charming*, I thought. I asked if this was their version of Halloween, and he said that he did not know what that was. His friend Ivan came with us. Ivan brought his friend, who was a girl, with him. His brother and his wife also went with us. While we were there walking down the sidewalk, a man started talking to us. Victor introduced him as Petar, a friend of his. He spoke very good English, just like Victor's other friend Ivan. Petar had very good computer skills.

The festival of the dead in the village was mainly a carnival with rides and people selling things like jewelry and candy. We went on some rides and had photos taken by his friend Ivan.

The next day, we took a long walk to the other side of the village because he said he had a surprise for me. While on this long walk, I had to pee in the bushes—lovely.

By the time we finally got there, I was in awe of what I saw. There out in the middle of the field were beautiful white Lipizzan horses, some with drawn carriages. Victor asked one of the horse owners if I could sit in the carriage so he could take a picture. The photo resembled that of a fairy tale. The horses would parade around the field in a circle for about an hour. It was beautiful. He knew I loved horses.

On our way home, Victor suggested that we stop and meet some people that he knew. I found out that he mostly did agricultural jobs for people he knew in the village and for very little pay. I would go with him most of the time. The people would feed him plus pay him the equivalent of ten dollars for six to eight hours of hard labor.

The customary beverage in his country was unfiltered coffee served very hot in teacups, served with either plum brandy, cola, or mineral water.

On hot sweltering days, I found out that they do not buy ice for their beverages. Their country did not sell ice either. According to Victor, you had to make your own ice at home, but very few people did. People there considered ice, fans, and air conditioners to be bad for the brain and cause headaches.

Drinking hot scalding coffee on a scorching one-hundred-degree day did not open my third eye.

One day, I was standing outside, and I said out loud, "Where's the beef?"

Victor said that there was none, which was a lie. Then not a few minutes later, did I hear a cow next door. I said, "There's the beef!"

Victor laughed and said, "Cows here are only used for milking."

I guess I was having cultural shock. In his country, the main meat staples are pork, chicken, and fish. I would eventually find butcher shops that sold beef. I also figured out that he did not like beef.

All day, I heard an owl. I asked Victor why owls were out during the day in his country, and he told me that they were not owls. They were doves.

Victor one day sat me down behind his computer and put a CD in and told me to sit there and watch it. He left the room while I watched. It was very strange indeed! It contained many men in black robes who kept reciting the same phrases repeatedly. Seven years later, I would research it and find out it was a Golden Dawn ritual. Whether it was a love spell or a mind-controlling ritual of some kind, I do not know. My guess is, it was a bit of both.

It is possible to control the thoughts and actions of another to have them do as you wish. Being controlled and manipulated by another human being is evil.

When you realize that someone has taken your free will and it wears off, you can become very angry and downright hostile. Victor did say things to me at the beginning of our relationship that were repetitive. I did not see or recognize any of this until much later in the relationship.

Victor's friend Ivan came to visit us one day to take more photos of Victor and I together for keepsake. While he was there, Victor got down on one knee and proposed while presenting me with a flat silver band. His friend Ivan took many photos of this event that I would later refer to as the US immigration engagement prop photos.

As I looked back at them, it was obvious that they were staged for US immigration purposes to document our relationship. For me, our relationship was genuine in the beginning. It did, however, go south at lightning speed as the years went by. I was not even finally divorced yet, and I was already engaged! I was being swept off my feet. Looking back on that event, it should have been another *red flag*.

Our four weeks together were coming to an end soon, and it would be time for me to return to the United States according to his country's immigration laws. I obeyed his country's immigration laws because as an American, I felt it was my responsibility. I also paid a lot over the years in foreign immigration fees to be in his country legally. I had to leave the next day. Victor cried all night. He said, "I am going to miss you so much, sweetie!" When Victor said sweetie, it sounded like sveetie.

I suggested that we spend our last night happy and not sad. I told him I would return when my divorce was settled.

In hindsight, I should have realized that after an eight-week courtship, getting engaged was not the smartest thing I've ever done. I thought I was in love.

On my return journey during my international travel flight, I noticed I was very agitated and short-tempered with the British Airways flight attendants and the airport agents. When I boarded my flight, I could not get to the overhead because the male flight attendant was blocking my way. I asked him if he could please put my bag into the overhead. He said, "No, but you can!"

I said, "Can you say dink!"

While going through customs at Heathrow Airport in London, the male customs agent took my hair conditioner. "But you're bald!" I said. The guy behind me was laughing his *ass* off.

For the rest of my flight back to the United States, I just sat in my seat and chilled. I felt like I was leaving the fourteenth century and going back to the twenty-first century. Seeing another culture for the first time was an eye-opener.

I had to go to divorce court the next day of my return, and I did not feel as though I had enough time to prepare, so I knew it would not go over well; nonetheless, I would continue just the same. Come what may.

CHAPTER 4

Second Thoughts

It was now mid-June, and having to go back to court to me at that time was not going to be very pleasant, but then again, is it ever? We were ordered by the judge to go attend mediation since we could not come to a suitable compromise on our own. I just sat there nice and calm and negotiated the split of an eighteen-year relationship. It was not an easy task.

During mediation, the only thing we mutually agreed on was the parenting of our seventeen-year-old daughter. This man who I had a child with and knew for about eighteen years did not want to provide me with anything after a twelve-year marriage even though the judge told him that I was entitled to some things. When he was asked about spousal support, he proceeded to stroke an invisible phallus in front of the mediator. He was a colorful character. That's why I spent the best years of my life with him.

I guess he had no clue that the mediator goes back to the judge with her report. She told me immediately after my ex's derogatory expression that I could leave and for him to stay behind with her. While I was walking out to my car, my skirt fell down around my ankles. If you want to lose weight, just get divorced.

The mediator took that to be a hostile and somewhat violent gesture toward me. He did have a propensity for the outrageous. I gave him three chances at reconciliation, and he blew all three chances. That is why I filed a petition for divorce. I was done! He had no right to be consumed with bitterness because he was the one who created it in the first place.

It is said that parting is such sweet sorrow, nonetheless very necessary to one's mental health. I had to let him go even though on some level, I still loved him. He did not want to give me anything, so I gave him everything I had, including our daughter and my personal injury settlement from my auto accident, which he fought for throughout our divorce proceedings relentlessly. I even sent our daughter monthly child support checks until her nineteenth birthday.

One night, I had a nightmare while my daughter was visiting with her father that weekend. I saw him walk into my bedroom and stab me with a knife until I was dead. When three other people that I knew also had the same premonition, I knew it was time for me to go.

What really freaked me out about that were the news reports of other homicides in town around that time. Those murders were all from husbands killing their soon-to-be ex-wives. Was it something in the water, or was someone putting these images into my mind?

From that point on, I started lying low, so no one knew where I was. Three months later, I boarded a bus and flew back across the pond to be with Victor. Although I did have second thoughts about it, I defaulted on my own divorce to start a new life.

CHAPTER 5

The Hesitant Bride

After reading an article on Yahoo about a vampire who was on the loose in one of the villages in Victor's country, I was hesitant, but I returned nonetheless in September 2010.

One day, I was sitting there all alone in our room when I heard something. I saw a mouse haul *ass* across the floor. I wanted to scream, but I'm not that much of a screamer unless I'm angry. I would later find out that Victor's mother's house had mice, flies, and spiders in the walls. I was not surprised. She had feral cats too that were breeding like jackrabbits. What a nightmare! I found a cat outside one day walking down the sidewalk with two broken back legs, and I brought it inside our room to ward off mice and take care of it.

Victor had me come along with him one day to see what he did to make money. I watched as he worked with a machine that separated corn from its cob. After they had the loose corn, they would put it into bags. Most of it was sold, the rest they kept so they could feed their own animals. The corn husks were used and sold as an alternative to wood used in woodstoves to cook and for warmth.

When Victor took a break from working, we were invited to have lunch. While we were sitting there in a room with a swarm of flies eating lunch, I said to Victor, "This is charming. What's with all the flies?"

One of the other guys asked Victor what I said. When he told the other guy what I said, the other guy asked, "Don't they have flies in the United States?"

I said, "Only when there's a pile of shit or a dead body nearby!"

Victor only made the equivalent of ten dollars for eight hours of work from those agricultural jobs. He also told me that people who had steady jobs in his country only made two-hundred and seventy-five dollars a month for pay.

Victor's country had more flies than you could shake a swatter at. It was because of the animals that they raised for food. It also had something to do with people making their own alcohol. It is the most horrible smell I've ever experienced—the smell of fermented fruit being cooked. I once joked with him that his country's national bird should be the fly.

Victor was associated with the firefighters in his village. He brought me to one of their annual track-and-field outings. I cheered him on from the sidelines while he ran like a gazelle being chased by a lion. He was able to scale and jump a ten-foot wall.

One time, we were invited to a benefit dinner being hosted by the firefighters. Not wanting to offend my host, I ate my soup that had fish heads in it looking at me. I closed my eyes and went to a happy place. I was on the beach, sipping a strawberry and mango margarita.

We traveled by bus to the next village. I went to an ATM to get money to buy food and other things. Exchanging American dollars for foreign currency became a new learning experience for me. Euros were more of equal value to American dollars than the local currency was. Sometimes I would gain 30 percent, and sometimes I would lose 30 percent on the value of every dollar. The ATMs there did not have decimals or commas. When I wanted to take out a hundred dollars, it looked something like this, 10000 instead of 100.00. When the local currency came out of the machine, it looked like I was being given ten thousand dollars. I thought to myself, *I really don't have that much money in my account.* I wish I did. I felt like I hit the lottery.

Victor and I went to the farmers market for food and personal items once or twice a week. We would relax in a coffee shop afterward while waiting for the next bus back home. The barmaid was a nice Hungarian woman who spoke very little English. I bought a couple of bottles of red wine from her one time. The wine was very good.

Victor and I enjoyed barbeque, soup, stuffed peppers with fresh bread, salmon, river fish, and tort desserts. Whenever I made an American recipe, he didn't seem to like it.

Victor and his family did not celebrate Christmas in the traditional way like Americans did. Their way of celebrating it was just dinner, no gifts—not that I was expecting anything. They just have different traditions. They celebrated two New Years and two Christmases because of the Catholic and Orthodox faiths. During the winter holidays, they have fireworks. They also celebrated Easter at two different times, again revolving around the Catholic and Orthodox faiths.

Over the years, I would only learn to speak very basic greetings of Victor's language. He would tell people that his language was too heavy for me to learn. He did nothing to teach me. Instead, he learned how to speak English but not that good in the beginning. He did get better over the years. I enjoyed using big words that I knew he would not understand. When he spoke English with a European accent, it was hard to understand. I would have to ask him to repeat it all the time. I remember the times when he would say to me that I did not speak proper English! Excuse me! Really? How can I not speak proper English when it is the only language I know? Besides a little French I took in middle school and a little Spanish I learned on the job.

Victor's friends would tell him that it was not right that he did not teach me his language. It made sense to me though because if I understood what they were saying, I probably would not have stayed in this relationship for as long as I did. Maybe he was trying to keep his nefarious intentions from me. It just felt that way. It brought back childhood memories of my paternal grandparents speaking only fluent French so the grandkids could not understand what they were saying.

Despite this obstacle, I either communicated with Victor's family, friends, and the locals with the basic greetings, or I just didn't say anything. It was kind of lonely and isolating. I would also find out later that those I thought could only speak the foreign language could, in fact, speak and understand English, which I thought was very deceptive.

Victor farted one morning and made a face like he had done something that was so horrible. I asked him what was wrong, and he told me that he was so ashamed that he just had wind from his *ass*. I never thought of it that way, but that was a very accurate description.

After two Christmases and two New Years, Victor started to discuss marriage plans. It was getting close to my birthday. My divorce was finalized the day before my birthday, which gave me a reason to celebrate a little extra that year. I was a little hesitant and felt like I needed more time because I wanted to heal from the first failed marriage before jumping so quickly into another one.

According to Victor, my engagement ring was not good enough, so it was time to go wedding ring shopping. Little did I know that I was going to be footing the bill for the two gold band wedding rings. Therefore, they were flat and plain. He would later demand that we go and get new ones that he was happy with that cost more and had a better turn-in value.

Still hesitant to get married again, I was none too pleased when I discovered that I was expected to pay for the whole thing, but I kept my outrageous disappointments to myself. I knew Victor was poor. I also understood why he wanted to go to the United States.

On Valentine's Day, Victor's brother murdered two pigs outside. The sound of them screaming as he was slitting their throats with a knife was horrifying. After the pigs were slaughtered and gutted, they were hung upside down. This was a horrifying sight to see.

Victor took the liberty to pick his best man and my maid of honor. They went with us to pick out his tux and my gown. Victor would not come out of the changing room after he saw me in the dress that I picked out and tried on. He would later confess that he had a hard-on from seeing me in my dress. Perhaps that was our bad luck or at least the beginning of it. Maybe Victor himself was feeling a bit hesitant about the whole thing.

We went to the registry to apply for our marriage license, and we were given a March date. We knew each other for about one year before we married. I did not sleep at all the night before the ceremony. Neither did he. I had some major doubts. My intuition was talking to me, and it had a lot to say. Apparently, I did not listen to my intuition, and I paid a very steep price for it.

My maid of honor did my hair in a very strange way that I found to be extremely unattractive. She colored my hair blond, and it came out orange. I was not a happy bride-to-be. I looked old and haggard and was hesitant and far removed from the whole thing. I didn't feel like I was even there. I was literally a ghost in my own life.

My sister-in-law kept making hand gestures to bring to my attention that I needed to smile for the wedding pictures. I thought perhaps I was just conflicted in my emotions—maybe even physically exhausted from only four hours of sleep that night. Looking back on those pictures, they told a story of a thousand words. I looked like someone had dimmed my *fucking* shine!

Although I did love Victor in the beginning of our relationship, it was very short-lived. Even though I had an English translator, I did not pay a single ounce of attention to what was being said. The piece of paper that was given to us after the ceremony, I could not read. It was in a foreign language that I did not understand fluently. When we went outside, every one threw coins at our feet. I threw my bouquet of red roses to Ivan's girlfriend, whom I believe would later marry someone who wasn't Ivan.

During the celebration dinner, Victor cut his hand, trying to open his brother's beer bottle. My maid of honor was the one to fix his wound and stop the bleeding, not me, you know, "the wife!" He picked out a song for us to dance to as husband and wife: Bryan Adams, "Everything I do, I do It for You!"

Victor's friend Ivan left his girlfriend at our reception to go across the village to tag the village pump. I thought that was low class. His mother did not attend our wedding ceremony, and she did not join us for the celebration dinner.

Aside from all that, it was a big blur for me. On our wedding day, I was too numb to stop the horrific tragedy that was taking place. I did not feel like I had any control over it at all. Every time I tried to talk, nothing came out. I tried to cry, but no tears would flow.

CHAPTER 6

The Twilight Zone Years

Our marriage consisted of me supporting my under employed spouse. I bought him clothes, paid our bills, and bought food. I lost a lot of weight in six years because Victor did not drive, so I walked a lot. Being lazy was not an option.

It was spring outside by now, and Victor asked me if I could buy some outdoor patio furniture so we could sit outside.

Allow me to describe what his yard looked like. It was muddy with many chickens, ducks, geese, and turkeys walking around free eating garbage and *shitting* all over the place—garbage everywhere, feathers, bugs galore, and a lovely view of the *shit* shack. Charming! Does that sound like something you would want to sit in and hang out? I think not! I didn't! I closed my eyes and went back to a time when I had my own yard, and how I worked hard on my days off from work to make it enjoyable. It was beautiful—with lush green grass, vegetable and flower gardens, the waterfall fountain I made with my own two hands, the gazebo my ex made, and the giant windchimes I hung in it, the hammock I used to spend time in relaxing while looking up at the sky, and the pool I put up for my daughter to enjoy all summer long. Then I opened my eyes to my current reality and realized that it was all just a dream.

I always thought Victor's ways were grandiose with a strange sense of entitlement. His whole family was that way, so it didn't surprise me that he was too. His mother would send one of the kids to knock on our door, asking for toilet paper. I would say, "Since you don't have a toilet, I don't have toilet paper." Sometimes sugar, "Sorry, I don't use sugar." Sometimes coffee, "Sorry, all out!" Victor did not work, so I didn't feel obligated to support his family also.

One day while we were out walking, Victor suggested that we stop by his best man's house.

Victor's best man brought us for a ride. He would bring us down to the riverside. I walked around, looking at the green river while the two of them discussed how to approach the American embassy in the capital of their country. They suggested that I file a petition for a family visa, so Victor could get a visa to the United States. I thought that it might be a wonderful idea considering I was homesick. I also thought that they must have been plotting this. I just didn't know for how long.

Two months after we were married, we went to the American embassy, so I could file a family visa petition. Every form and petition I filed had a fee. Two months later, we were called to come back for our petition and our application interviews. The interviews were demeaning and full of disrespectful remarks, more toward Victor than myself. The American consulate did point out some obvious things to me, such as why I thought Victor's first marriage had failed and why. I said it was because they were not compatible. I also knew it was because she didn't want to live in a dilapidated, run-down building with no toilet and no hot water. I knew this because that's how Victor's environment was. He did not have the means to support her because he did not work. At the very least, he did not have the means to support another person. He couldn't even support himself.

The English translator did such a poor job that it was difficult to understand the exact nature of the demise of his first marriage. Regardless of this, I did pick out many things that to me made sense. I did see that some of their issues became ours as well, such as different life views, frequent misunderstandings, and lack of financial support from Victor.

The translator of our documents was also the translator at our wedding, and she pulled me aside one day and said to me, "I hope you have rainy-day savings just in case." She told me I would probably need it at some point in this marriage. She went so far as to suggest that I get a job in the village teaching English at the school. I had income. "Victor is the one that needs a job," I told her.

The more I thought about that statement from her though, the more I came to understand that her translation of Victor's previous marriage document was not accurate unless the reader knew his native language because the American version was repetitive. She could have also been reluctant to put the truth in English. Maybe she was threatened. I don't know. That also could have been behind the questions from the American consulate.

We passed the family petition interviews at the US embassy. I had to help Victor fill out his visa application, which told me that he was not very bright and did not really have any work experience, education, or that he was just lying about things. During our interview, after all the immigration forms were filled out and paid for by me, of course, it was discovered that I did not have enough income to support Victor's bid for a US visa. I did not meet the financial requirements of immigration form I-864, affidavit of support.

I was relieved but disappointed at the same time. I wanted to go home and not have to live in a Third World country. There were many reasons why Victor's visa should have been denied and the marriage dissolved. It was all beginning to unravel.

The American consulate asked Victor if he had any assets. Victor told him that all his assets were in his mother's name. The American consulate shot me a look of, "What does that tell you?" That told me that my marriage was based on lies and that I was probably being used for a green card. From that moment on, I would make sure that Victor never got a green card or entered the United States of America.

Victor told me when we first met that he owned his mother's house and a cornfield. He lied to me. He told me not long after that that he would never consider putting his property up for collateral for a US visa. He wanted all this to be on my dime! Yeah, not going to happen, slick.

We left the US embassy that day, and Ivan drove us to his house because it was close by. While we were all sitting down having a drink, company arrived to see Ivan's mother. Ivan suggested that I follow him into another room to talk shop about his old car that was in his garage. Victor and Ivan's mother spoke with this unknown woman who had her four-year-old daughter with her. Could that woman have been Victor's ex-wife? Was that child Victor's daughter? I don't know for sure. It is only speculation on my part. His divorce from his first wife was in 2007. Why was I taken from the room then?

Because I couldn't speak their language, I didn't know what was going on. All I knew was that it was a strange event, like everything else I experienced in this twilight zone life I found myself living.

The US embassy sent him a denial letter in the mail two months later. His friends and family were not too thrilled. If he was not going to the United States, then neither were they.

I started to research all I could about the United States visa laws, and I found out that they do not protect the American citizen. It only protects the foreign national spouse. I found out that if his visa was approved, he could have come to the United States, and after two years, he would have been able to get a green card, divorce me, and legally be entitled to financial support from me. Those are some of our immigration laws that I found to be unacceptable and a serious game changer as far as this relationship was concerned.

Victor was angry about his US visa denial, and he threw his passport into the woodstove.

A week later, Victor reapplied for a new passport. Guess who had to pay for that too? You guessed it, me! The financial abuse was never-ending. If Victor could not come to my country and be supported by me, then he was content to have me live in his country and support him while he drained every penny of my monthly income.

At this point, I realized that I was doomed to live in a Third World country while being financially and psychologically mistreated, which took a huge toll on my physical and emotional well-being.

I got sick of boiling a big pot of water on the woodstove, so I could wash key areas of my body. His mother called it, "Making shower."

I told her, "You don't make a shower. You take a shower."

Victor went out and bought a used hot water heater. After mounting it to the wall, he discovered the heating element didn't work and needed to be replaced. Guess who bought a brand-new heating element? Me! Now I could at least take a hot shower and wash my clothes by hand in the shower cabin. His mother did not feel any need or obligation to pay for the hot water heater that I put in her house. She would also ask me for money and other things but never felt that she had to pay me back for anything, yet every time Victor borrowed a few bucks off her, which was not very often, she always expected me to pay her back immediately. I thought that was scummy. I called her scummy mummy. These creatures were taking total advantage of me.

One day, Victor told me that he needed to help our best man and maid of honor with their family's agricultural machine. They wanted me to watch their kids. Not really into babysitting but I went reluctantly. This was around seven months after we were married.

While the adults were outside working, I was sitting there, watching foreign television that I could not understand. I felt something hit the back of my head. I turned around, and their four-year-old daughter was spitting on the back of my head from behind the couch. I said, "Did you just spit at me?"

She said to me in plain English (which she could only have learned or heard from the adults like her mother, father, grandfather, and Victor), "Stupid fucking American. You will never be his wife, and you will never have his children." I really didn't need to hear this from a four-year-old child; however, this was the confirmation I needed to hear in order to validate that Victor only married me for a green card. It made me even more determined to see that he would never get one. I stood up and walked out in a fit of rage.

When Victor saw me walk by him and leave the property, he followed me and asked me what was wrong. I told him everything. I also told him to go *fuck* himself and his sham of a marriage! He followed me all the way back to his mother's *shit* hole house while the whole time he got to witness my rage. He did not say a word other than the child must have heard this on television. "No!" I told him. "She heard it from all of you shit bag adults!"

I know I should have divorced Victor immediately after that incident. It would have saved me the extra grief, heartache, and financial abuse in the long run.

One night, I had a nightmare that I was running from room to room inside his mother's house, and some woman was following me from room to room. She stood in the shadow near the door, so I could not see her. In my nightmare, I came right out and asked her, "Who are you?" The voice I had sounded like a dead person, a ghost. In my nightmare, I saw myself spitting up blood clots. She stepped out of the shadows for just a second, but all I could see was a middle-aged woman with big cheeks and shoulder-length dark hair. I did not know who she was. I never saw her before.

Victor woke me up after he heard me talking in my sleep. Our cat looked at me and bolted from the bed.

I told Victor that I would be returning to the United States. He told me to obtain an immigration attorney and increase my income. I had to get out of there. I was coming unglued.

In the morning, I went outside to hang some of my clothes up, I saw two guys from next door sitting in their truck with a view above the wall laughing at Victor's mother, who was standing there totally naked! What the *fuck*! I hung my clothes and went back inside. I always knew there was something fundamentally wrong with this woman.

Two weeks later, we went to the capital to get my international flight tickets. While we were sitting in an outside café, I saw a young couple a few tables over who were in love and could not keep their hands off each other. All Victor could talk about was me getting an immigration attorney for him. It suddenly hit me like a ton of bricks that not only was the honeymoon over, but it may not have even been real in the first place. What blew my mind was that he slept very well at night—not me. I tossed, turned, snored, and had nightmares like someone who was in deep turmoil.

It took five planes to reach my destination in the United States. Within two days, I had a job cleaning hotel rooms even though I had office skills. I went to see an immigration attorney who was an immigrant herself. I allowed this endeavor to fall through the cracks because I did not want Victor to get a US visa. During this time, he demanded that I give him the immigration attorney's contact information. Victor contacted me on Skype and allowed his mother to sit there looking at me while she was crying. *Emotional abuse*, I thought. I don't have to take this, so I clicked on the sign-out button.

One day, that was my day off from work, I went into a CVS Pharmacy and noticed I was feeling a bit off—dizzy with an impending sense of doom. I sat down at one of those blood pressure cuff machines and found out my pressure was 180/142. The pharmacist asked me if I wanted her to call an ambulance. I told her I would just take a taxi. I had a massive kidney infection.

I would later find out that I also had a tumor on my right adrenal gland that was growing and causing high and low blood pressure. I am sure severe stress played a role also. Five airplane flights probably didn't help much either.

During this time, Victor would demand that I see and talk to him on Skype. He kept pushing me to do what he wanted when he wanted. I told him that I was not feeling well, yet he did not seem to give a *shit*! I told him to go *fuck* himself. I did not talk to or see him for days after that. He had his United States Facebook female friends call my phone. I never picked up my phone, so they never had the chance to harass me either, like they had done before. He kept sending me e-mails saying that I had to apply for a name change on my passport. I mailed my application and waited for a response.

A week later, I received a letter telling me that I needed to return to my home state to find out the nature of why my passport was being suspended by the State Department. I returned to New England a week later to investigate the matter. I lived with a relative for about four weeks before going off again on my own to take care of personal matters. I found myself living in some not so nice conditions; however, it was all I could afford at the time, and the location was perfect. After finding out that I owed around a little under $5,000 in child support from my 2011 divorce, I made it my personal mission to correct the situation by going through the proper channels.

I found out that the State Department cannot suspend your passport for less than $5,000. I was at $4,012. I thought maybe they considered me to be a flight risk.

Everything I needed was within walking distance, so I spent many days filling out paperwork and setting up appointments and a court date.

Apparently, my ex neglected to notify state child support that I was sending our daughter child support the whole time I was across the pond and still upon my return. I was not too surprised by this. At the time, I could not afford to hire a family lawyer, so I had to be my own lawyer. I spent every day, all day at the Nashua library going through law books, looking for my angle on how to win my case. While I was at the library one day, I noticed that my America online account (AOL) had been hacked into. I had lost access to my account. I tried to go into my Facebook page also and found out that someone had hacked that too. I could not change my password, so I contacted Facebook and told them to delete my account.

Apparently, Victor had taken over my accounts, and he was writing things and posting pictures of our wedding all over my page according to friends. All this because I was too busy to spend all day and all *fucking* night on Skype!

It was around the beginning of July, and by that time, I had lost sixty pounds in three months. Most of my income went toward keeping a roof over my head, which only left enough money for a five-hundred calorie a day diet, plus I walked on average about two to three miles a day. I didn't have a car. I gave up my American life for a man who had no means. Even though I was in the United States without Victor, I still felt isolated, manipulated, and controlled.

During that July heat wave of 2012, I took a walk to Dunkin' Donuts to get a large iced tea. While I was there, I checked my e-mail because the place I lived at did not have wireless internet. My Skype popped up, and there was Victor looking madder than a wet hen. While I was sitting in a public place, he decided he was going to let me have it with both barrels for not keeping in touch with him over the past several weeks. I asked him how he expected me to be in touch with him if he hijacked my social media. I noticed that he was not a rational individual. This was not the man I met and fell in love with two years ago.

I was sitting in Dunkin' Donuts, and Victor was yelling at me at the top of his lungs on Skype. People started giving me dirty looks. I started yelling back at Victor. We went at it like two rabid dogs for ten minutes. Then we settled down and had a calm conversation.

In the corner sat a table of Calcutta Indians who were speaking in their native tongue. There was something about hearing a bunch of people speaking in a language that I did not understand that set me off completely. It reminded me of my life with Victor in a foreign country, and my brain started to explode like a bomb. I started to become extremely agitated, and I started to cry. I excused myself to go into the restroom to get my emotions under control. I left my laptop on with Victor on Skype. I figured no one would steal it because he was looking right at them. I noticed I was just not feeling right. Victor told me to go back to my room and lie down. *Good idea*, I thought, so I said goodbye. Then I walked the two miles back and up three flights of stairs. When I got into my room, I sat down on the metal chair next to the window.

My left arm went numb and electric fence tingly and dropped to my side. Then I could not feel the left side of my head. I was sitting there, looking out the window with a view of the hospital, so I decided to start walking down there. Something was seriously wrong. To make a long story short, I had a stroke, and I was in the hospital for four days. During those four days, I was treated by the head doctor, who was a Romanian woman. I told her that I was married but separated from my husband, who was from a country close to her homeland. We exchanged our experiences with US immigration. A neurologist came in to talk to me. I asked him if he was from Poland. He told me he was from Belarus. The next morning, a Russian neurologist came into my room to talk to me. What country am I in? *I must be in the twilight zone*, I thought.

I recovered without any major damage, or so I thought. It did, however, take me many weeks to get back up to my normal walking pace.

At a time in my life when I really needed someone, I was completely alone. My mother called my cell phone. I answered and told her I was in the hospital. She came up to see me. I don't know how or why I survived it. Victor called too to find out why he could not contact me yet again for many days. I told him what had happened to me that day. He seemed only the slightest bit concerned.

I moved to a nicer place close by, and to my amazement, it was near a bus station. Now I could go places and not have to walk. While I was still preparing for my court case, I would talk to Victor on Skype in the library. He told me to go to the DMV to renew my license and change my name. Victor never asked me to do anything. He either told me, or he demanded that I do what he said. It is very out of character for me to be so gullible and complying.

The next morning, I set out on a walk to the DMV. The bus apparently did not have a stop close enough. I stopped at Dunkin' Donuts for a vanilla iced coffee to fuel my three-mile round-trip journey. While I was getting my coffee, a man fell to the floor. Because he looked like a homeless bum, no one helped him. I ran over to help him. I believe he was having a seizure. I looked up at the employees standing behind the counter, just staring out into space, and I yelled for someone to call for an ambulance. While I was walking, I could hear the sirens on their way. It started to rain. The rain turned into a torrential downpour, and I got soaked. I never got a driver's license that had a good photo of me. Who does? This photo was memorable because I was sixty pounds lighter and literally soaking wet.

Despite having a stroke two months prior and no legal representation, I won my court case! I should have gone to law school. I probably would have had a better life.

Victor pressured me to return across the pond in the second week of December. He had filled my head with so much nonsense that I couldn't think straight in an attempt to get me to return to him. I hated him for that because he took me away from an event in my life that was supposed to be a happy one. Because of his selfishness, controlling and manipulative ways, I was denied that joy. He ripped me out of my daughter's life for the third time in three years.

I had been in the United States for eight months. I had to fight in court to get the child support charges dropped. I would not fault, and I did not waiver until I presented all my evidence. All those days, weeks, and months spent in the library learning from law books paid off! I discovered that I could accomplish anything I set my mind to. I was a force to be reckoned with. Once that was handled then, I could apply for another passport with a name change.

When I returned to Victor, he was cold and unfeeling. I was extremely upset because of what I gave up yet again for another round of his abuse. He said to me that people who have stokes end up with distorted faces. He had it stuck in his head that while I was in the United States for eight months that I cheated on him. My body was with me the whole time, and I would know if I cheated or not. Usually, people accuse you of something that they themselves are guilty of. His demeanor toward me was becoming a great concern.

One night, he had to go to the emergency room. His face turned white. He had passed a kidney stone.

A week or so later, Victor told me that he was interested in taking an online certificate course to gain a job skill. He said it would benefit our future. During this time, he was taking total advantage of me, and I was still trying to fully recover from having a stroke. He wanted to study web design and business English from some online college. I supported his endeavor just like I did when I paid for him to finish high school.

Victor and his mother incurred a big food bill with a village merchant, and guess who had to pay for that? Me! The woman who owned the store spoke very good English, and she was always nice to me.

Victor did odd jobs for other people in the village. They would sometimes knock on the outside of our bedroom window.

While I was sleeping one morning, an older woman came pounding on the window so loud that I woke up out of a dead sleep, stumbled due to dizziness, then fell to the floor, hitting my head. I got back up and opened the window, and I said to her, "If you ever knock on my fucking window again, I will come outside and personally kick your ass!" I said that because I thought she didn't understand English. When I told Victor about the incident, he told me that she did understand English.

By this time, Victor's brother moved out and into his new girl-friend's house. He was divorced and took custody of his three kids. My ex-sister-in-law wanted her own home. Can't blame her. Living with the mother-in-law in her dilapidated building was creepy. The mother had a bunch of feral cats that were infested with fleas. She slept with two of them. Victor told me that while I was in the United States, our cat died crossing the road, and it was all my fault. How was that my fault?

One day, Victor asked me if I could please help his mother walk to the doctor down the sidewalk and into the village, which was about a fifteen-minute walk. I asked him why he could not do this, and he said of his own mother that she was disgusting! I walked her to the doctor's office. While we were sitting there waiting for her to see the doctor, I saw fleas and something else crawling all over her head.

It became quite apparent to me that I was now infested with fleas. I stood up and walked out. I went home to take a shower. I had fleabites all over my arms and legs. I took pictures with my cell phone. My cell phone became broken. Victor did not want anyone to see how much of an evil piece of *shit* he truly was.

The following September, I was admitted into the hospital for heavy blood loss due to a female medical condition. While I was there, I also needed a blood transfusion. The day I was going to be released, Victor came into my room and told me that he needed me to walk across the street with him to the ATM because he needed money. I found this to be a bit concerning. I was angry. Apparently, I had to pay my bill for my hospital room before they would take the IV out of my hand.

I wrote a poem that adequately described the condition of the inside of Victor's mother's house. When he found the poem I wrote, he became very upset and destroyed it. He did not want people to know how poor he was and how much of a raw deal his wife had. I did, at one point, take pictures of his mother's house and her yard with the intention of posting them online. He destroyed my cell phone. I still have a picture of the outside of his mother's house that I took in the very beginning of our relationship.

I found out that his best man had taken a job with a Canadian company, driving and delivering frozen fish by truck all over the United States. Victor told me that his best man wanted to better deal his wife. *What a cad*, I thought.

I paid several hundred for Victor to go to driver's education school, and I bought him a car—one that he picked out.

Victor's friend Ivan came over to look at the car because he was an auto mechanic. When there was no one else around, he decided to insult me. I said to him, "You don't have what it takes to insult me!" That was the last time I ever saw him.

No matter what I did to make our lives better, I knew deep down inside that I was being used only to make Victor's life better.

When we tried to make a garden together, Victor was too much of an *asshole* for me to continue to work with him. Victor accused me of murdering his pumpkins, so he murdered my avocado plant and blamed it on the goat. I continued to garden without him. I grew beets, lettuce, cucumbers, potatoes, tomatoes, scallions, squash, and carrots. Every morning, I would go outside at dawn and weed my garden before it got too hot to continue. I would bring in some fresh raspberries and put them in the freezer for a cool healthy snack when it was hot outside.

I noticed several marijuana plants in his mother's garden that were mixed in with the potatoes. Victor told me that his brother put them there. He would come along and chop them down because he was afraid that he would get blamed. Victor told me one time that his brother got caught with them in the family garden and told the police that they were Victor's. At the time, Victor was in another country. Helicopters went over the village, looking for illegal marijuana plants.

After watching the 1978 movie *Midnight Express*, about the American guy who was arrested for possession of hashish and ended up spending twenty-five years in a Turkish prison, I wanted nothing to do with anyone's garden pot plants.

His mother asked him to cut the grass, so he went into the shed and out he came with a scythe. I laughed, and I said, "What are you, the Grim Reaper?"

I ended up buying Victor a weed-whacker. He turned it into a way for him to make some money and keep his own lawn looking good. I am referring to the lawn outside the gate.

Every time I had to go to the doctors, they would yell at Victor and tell him that he was negligent of my health. I had to have an EKG at the doctor's office one time because my blood pressure was very high. That was when Victor told them about my stroke. The doctor gave me a half pill to bring down my blood pressure, then she gave me a prescription. She also sent me to see a neurologist who also gave me a prescription for something else. The neurologist could also tell that my stroke happened on my right side by the way I walked.

When I had to go to the emergency room at the hospital for my high blood pressure concerns, the US embassy told me that the hospitals in this country were not up to Western hospital standards, and they were not kidding.

There were no doors in the emergency rooms. While I was lying there during the EKG with no shirt or bra on, everyone sitting out in the waiting room could see my boobs. I closed my eyes and went to a happy place, which was a beautiful beach and a peach margarita.

Although I was literally falling apart on my way home from the hospital, I decided to go to a travel agent and see about getting a vacation package. I needed to get the hell out of Dodge myself. It was starting to wear and tear on me.

CHAPTER 7

Aegean Sea

I put a vacation package on pay by the month layaway until thirty days prior to the start of our vacation. I chose to go to an exotic location in a beautiful country. I could not believe Victor had lived so close to there all his life and never gone.

I booked a twenty-day vacation package for a beach vacation, which was near the Aegean Sea. The cost of travel and vacation packages in Europe are cheaper than they are in the United States. I wanted to go to the southern part of this country, but the cost was too much. I have learned that if you want to travel to Europe, buy your plane ticket from a European travel agent instead of a United States travel agent. This can save you hundreds of dollars.

I found out two weeks prior to our vacation that his brother was moving back home because his girlfriend threw him and his three kids out. When he moved back home, I noticed he started to obtain a bunch of animals. Most people who lived around there raised their own animals for food. They will literally walk by you, grab a chicken, and cut the head off. When Victor suggested to me that I buy a bunch of animals, I said no! I don't have it in me to murder an animal, yet I have no problem buying their meat at the butchers or grocery store.

I cringed when I found out he was coming back because I knew he would get animals again. He got two pigs, two goats, several chickens, ducks, turkeys, and geese. It was the roosters that were irritating. American roosters make noise at sunrise. European roosters make noise from midnight to sunrise. I found it hard to sleep. I wanted to go outside and get the rooster and put it up to his brother's *ass*!

One day, Victor told me that his mother had to chase one of the goats that got loose all over the village. I thought that was funny. She never caught it.

I also found out from Victor that his brother threatened his girlfriend and her family, which did not surprise me because he did the same to his ex-wife and her family according to Victor. I found this to be a lie when his girlfriend showed up and started hanging around. She seemed like a nice lady, but in my book, any woman who slept with a married man was nothing but a low-life homewrecker.

If you do not want to be with your spouse anymore, you should end the marriage then take up with whoever you choose. I have zero respect for women like that although it is just as much the men's fault, if not more.

Anyway, I believe he was giving her a couple of turkeys to appease his guilt. I asked Victor if he could ask her where I could buy some clothes and footwear for my vacation since I did not have any decent clothes or sandals.

Victor decided he was going to be a *dink* that day that she took us shopping. When he did not get what he wanted, he was very childish. She took us to a store for clothes that were owned and operated by Chinese merchants. We found some good deals. Then she took us to a shoe store for some nice sandals. When I was done picking out my new sandals, Victor asked me if she could pick out a pair for taking us shopping. I said that it was okay.

We had coffee while the two of them spoke in their native language. I could not understand what they were saying. I always disliked being excluded from the conversation. Victor only knew a few people who could speak English. It bothered me that they still had a conversation in front of me that I could not understand.

Before our vacation, I noticed while watching television one day that we would be going during the height of the 2015 Greek austerity. I was a little nervous about that.

Vacation day came fast. Before I knew it, we were on a bus and heading south. The kid sitting behind me all twenty-four hours kept planting his knees into my spine.

In Europe, they do not call them hotels/motels. They refer to them as apartments. I found out that the kid that sat behind me on the bus was in the apartment on our right with his parents and brother.

On the ride down there, I enjoyed traveling through Macedonia. The roads went through the tunneled mountains. Although I was nervous looking out the window and how far the bus would fall if it went off the road, it was a beautiful country nonetheless.

I was disappointed when we got into Greece because it looked like a Third World country, and that is what I was trying to leave behind. When we finally got closer to our destination, it started to look less Third World. I could see the beautiful Aegean Sea in the distance. I always wanted to compare the Atlantic Ocean to the sea. I like the ocean much better. The food in Greece was expensive but very good.

When we got to our apartment, we were told that we had to wait before we could enter until the maids were done cleaning. I found out that if you wanted air-conditioning in your room, you had to pay extra by the day. I was not happy with that. I paid enough for the place for twenty days already. The building was owned by a woman from Victor's country who was married to a Greek man.

For the whole twenty days, her name is almost all I would hear my husband say to the point where it became borderline nauseating.

While we were waiting for our apartment, we decided to go down to the sea. I thought that the rocks on the bottom were very sharp. One of the locals suggested we try to follow the sand path out to avoid the sharp stones.

The Aegean Sea is turquoise blue from a distance, but when you get up close, it is green. When you wash your swimwear, it turns the wash water green.

After we went swimming, we started walking back to our apartment to see if it was ready yet. It was not, so we went to get a bite to eat. We had gyro sandwiches with a Coke. When our room was ready, we took a shower and a nap.

When Victor woke up, he wanted to go back to the sea. We spent the first week eating gyro sandwiches and going back and forth to the sea. Instead of putting sunblock on my back while it was a hundred degrees every day during the whole vacation, he was too busy twenty-five feet out diving for seashells. I did notice some strange things floating in the sea. I knew that Syrian refugees were coming from Turkey by boat to reach Greece. From there, they were making their journey up through Europe.

After a week of spending every day at the beach, I had a second-degree sunburn on my upper back and both shoulders. It became too painful to put on my bathing suit, yet all Victor wanted to do was go to the sea ten times a day. I had to take a couple days off from going to the sea. Every time he came back, he would bring back with him some woman. One woman he brought back to meet me said hello, and she also mentioned that she was married and had three kids. I said, "Then why are you hanging around with my husband if you are so happily married with three kids?"

Of course, she was speechless!

I did not receive medical attention until three days later. While the Greek female doctor was talking to me, her and my husband were making goo-goo eyes at each other. Fed up with all this *bullshit*, I just came right out and asked her to prescribe something for me so I could have some relief and get the hell out of there. Did he do this to me on purpose? I have no doubt.

Our vacation consisted of going to the sea back and forth from morning to night—either eating out or making gyros sandwiches back at our apartment. We also had fun buying some cool things to remind us of our vacation.

When the people whom Victor and I made friends with were getting ready to leave after their two weeks of vacation, he spent the night over at their outside terrace drinking plum brandy.

Victor came back at the end of the night and puked all over our bathroom. *Nice! Real fucking nice*, I thought. "Now you can clean it up!" He did a piss poor job, so naturally, I had to pick up the slack and finish. I wanted to smash his face in at this point.

Sadly, I have equated taking a vacation to getting *shit-faced* drunk. Both are intended to get away from low-vibing sketchy-*ass* people. Vacations and getting drunk are just a temporary fix. When you come down or return from vacation, you are right back where you started in the first place. That's when you realize that some serious changes need to be made in your life.

One night, I totally flipped out. I was so mad at Victor that I didn't want to be intimate. He wouldn't leave me alone, so I picked him up and threw him across the room over two double beds. He came up real slow on the other side of the mattress with a look of "Did she really just throw me across the room?" Victor, I believe, knew at that point that his *bullshit* was wearing extra thin.

I am not sure if Victor tried to destroy my vacation on purpose or if he was that much of a *dick*! Despite him, I enjoyed my Greek vacation because it was my first time in Greece, so just being able to be there was wonderful.

Victor would go out on the terrace every morning and talk to the other guests while I made us some coffee.

There was an older woman who used to walk by our apartment while I was sitting outside, and she would smile and nod. Another woman who lived across the street from us ran over and gave me a cold soda. She was a nice lady. Victor told me that she was Albanian.

One of our neighbors, the one with the kid that had his knees in my back all the way down there, asked me why the American embassy only employed mainly the natives and not Americans. I told him it was because they don't have to pay health insurance or a higher pay that they would have to pay an American. He asked me if I would like to babysit his kids, and I declined. I told him Victor would be more than happy.

Another gentleman told Victor and me about his walk up the hill to the mountain. He told us how beautiful it was up there. The next day, we set out on a different journey far from the sea. We had to walk all the way uphill to get there. The outside restaurant and bar that the man told us about were closed. It was like a ghost town.

Victor suggested that we continue up the road further. I had to reach down for that extra something because my legs were dead. We walked all the way uphill to a dead end. At the end of the road was a set of wooden stairs.

By that time, I literally felt as though I had died and was finally going to ascend my own stairway to heaven.

Victor was twenty-five feet ahead of me and halfway up the stairs. When I got to the beginning of the stairs, I was bitten by a large greenfly. From that point on, I started to move quickly up the stairway. At the top were Victor and some religious temple or shrine. Greek Orthodox would have been my guess. This holy shrine was plagued by biting giant flies, and in my opinion, we should not have been there. What a view though from that altitude! We could see the sea way down in the distance. We took a few pictures, then quickly left, and went down the hill and back to our apartment. Two days later, we were boarding our bus. I was not looking forward to returning to his house in the village. We arrived late that night, and he had to call his brother to come and pick us up. My sunburn, by the way, was not fully healed upon my return home. It took about four months to fully heal.

Our vacation to Greece gave me another reason to believe that our marriage was not doing well. The only glue for me that ever kept this relationship intact was the fire in the beginning that no longer existed. I had to come to terms with letting go. How hard could that have been knowing the circumstances? What was I holding onto? Was I afraid of having another failed marriage?

CHAPTER 8

Gutted Like a Fish

Victor asked me if we could go to the wine festival. I told him that we couldn't afford it. If he had a job and a car to drive up north, I would have loved spending my day sampling wine. My favorite wine in his country was Vranac. This was a very strong red wine.

Victor also came up with a reason why he could not obtain his driver's license. He said that he needed to have surgery on both his eyes because of an accident he had years ago. According to him, he had two detached retinas due to a head injury on the job. I could not afford $3,000 per eye. Neither could he. Why did his mother not take care of this years ago? She supported his brother, and he worked. She gave Victor's brother money. I was sick of being used, and I just was not having any more of it. I knew his mother was suggesting to him that I pay for all kinds of *shit*. I had no respect for her at all. I believed that he was just scamming me extra at that point.

One day, I started to break out into a cold sweat. I started to feel dizzy like if I did not sit down, I was going to fall. I sat down, and both my legs from the hips down went numb, and I could not move or stand up. I looked at him sitting on the bed, and I could barely utter the word help. He just sat there and looked at me like he was waiting for me to die or something. It took about thirty minutes to an hour for me to recover from whatever was happening to my body. When I was finally able to stand up, I went to go lie down.

One night not too long after that incident, I started to feel a really bad pain in my lower right abdominal. I thought it might be my right ovary or something. I told Victor that I needed to go to the hospital. He told me I probably just had some type of stomach flu. I passed out from the pain. In the morning, it was still there. I said to him, "Stomach flu my ass! I'm going to the doctors!"

Victor followed me all the way to the doctor's office, walking twenty-five feet behind me. The doctor pressed down on the pain, and she had to peel me off the ceiling. She said, "I want you to go to the emergency room immediately. You have appendicitis." A year before this, a friend of Victor's had died from his appendicitis because he waited too long to seek medical treatment.

When I arrived at the hospital, I was brought into the emergency room immediately so a doctor could assess my condition. He took his hands and pressed down the same as the other doctor did. I took my hands and removed his. The pain was unbearable. He turned around and yelled at Victor. I asked Victor, "What did the doctor say?" He told me that the doctor was angry because I was not brought to the hospital yesterday. Now I was starting to get nervous. I did not want to have surgery in a foreign country.

Victor was told to take me upstairs to the operating ward for surgery preparations. I was scared *shit*! I was brought into a room and told to lie on the bed. Victor was told to go home and come back tomorrow. I was in a foreign country, and the only person I knew could not be there for me.

A nurse came in to shave my pubic hair off with an ancient razor. I would later dub her the razor Nazi. She left the room after she was finished, then a male nurse came in and told me to follow him. I followed him to a room where he told me to take off my clothes and change into a substandard surgical gown. I was brought to another room for surgery. As I was lying on the table trying not to cry, the anesthesiologist came up from above me and put a cell phone to my ear and told me to talk to her English-speaking son who was going to ask me some questions that were important for me to answer prior to my surgery. I answered his questions, then she put a mask over my face. I don't recall how long the actual procedure took, but I remember waking up not being able to breathe. The anesthesia lady was smacking my face and saying, "Darlene, breathe. Darlene, wake up!"

I said to her, "I can't breathe!" I was barely able to get the words out. It felt like the wind was knocked out of me. She quickly put an oxygen tube in my nose. I believe I passed out.

I woke up in a room with two other female patients. The surgeon came in to see and asked me how I was feeling. I said, "Like I fell out of a hundred-story window and was run over by an eighteen-wheeler!" He just looked at me and walked out of the room. I don't believe that was the answer he wanted to hear, but nonetheless, that was the only description of how I felt.

When the nurses came into my room the next day to change my surgical dressing, I looked down at the incision, and I passed out at the sight of it. I believe the appendix is only a few inches long, yet they gutted me like a fish, and I was horrified. The nurses woke me up with some cold facecloths. Then they asked me to stand up. I said, "Are you fucking kidding me?" This was my seventh abdominal surgery, and the body can only take so much.

Two nurses grabbed my legs, and two grabbed my arms. They were going to sit me up and get me to stand. When they had me standing, my head kept falling toward the floor. They yelled at me to pick my head up. Then they walked me over to the sink near the doorway, where they held me up and told me to turn the water on and splash some cold water on my face. I did even though all I wanted to do was lay back down and finish dying. I asked one of the nurses why I had a surgical scar from my groin to way past my belly button. She told me she would send the surgeon in to talk to me.

A nurse came in to start intravenous therapy in my right hand. I found out that I did not have good veins for this, so it was very painful to endure. The nurse also gave me a shot in my stomach. The surgeon came in and told me that when he made a three-inch incision and saw what was going on, he had to open me up more. My appendix, my lower and upper abdominal cavity, was covered in gangrene/dead tissue.

Now I needed seven days of serious intravenous antibiotic therapy to clear sepsis from my blood. Could having sepsis explain the change to my mental status? Maybe. I was dying, and they saved my life.

I was told that if my appendix burst prior to surgery, I would have died. Victor came to see me two days after my surgery.

While Victor was there, he spoke to the woman on my right in his native language, so, of course, I didn't know what was being said as usual. That was a constant during my six years in his country. Before I went into the hospital that day, I did give Victor some money so he could eat while I was in the hospital. I noticed that he had on a new pair of sneakers.

Victor brought me some toilet paper. In his country, hospitals do not supply their bathrooms with it. You must bring your own. That was another constant in my life while I lived in his country. I asked Victor one time why his country did not supply toilet paper to the public, and he said it had something to do with the Gypsy population. These people were of Calcutta India decent. They did not work, and they did not go to school. They were thieves and full-time beggars.

After Victor left and went home, the patient he was talking to suddenly had a visitor from Victor's village. She told her visitor who I was married to, and she had a look of disgust on her face and a look of pity for me. Was there something that I did not know about my own husband? Maybe. I was starting to get a strange feeling about the whole thing.

After seven days of intravenous antibiotic therapy, I had run out of toilet paper, so I told one of the surgeons that came in to see me that it was time to discharge me from the hospital. I was out of bathroom supplies. He said, "Then send your husband to the bank to get more toilet paper."

I said, "I am the bank!"

"Oh," he said, "then I will bring you the discharge papers."

When I went home, I went to bed. In the morning, I got up and went to go to take a shower. I just stood there under the water and cried. When I felt like I was going to pass out, I would yell to Victor for help. He never came. It felt like my blood pressure was taking a dive. Luckily, I never passed out. I never wanted to be found naked in the shower cabin passed out or dead. That was always my biggest fear. I had dignity.

Victor would suggest to me every day that I go with him for a walk outside. I could not put on underwear or pants due to the incision. He never had abdominal surgery. I was depressed physically and emotionally. I fell back asleep after taking diclofenac, which is a European painkiller.

On the day that I had to go back to the hospital to have my stitches removed, the attending doctor took both hands and pushed down on my lower abdomen and yelled at Victor. I don't know what he said to him, but I could tell by his tone and by the look on Victor's face that it was not a good conversation between the two of them.

The doctor took my stitches out and told Victor to bring me to admitting. I had to endure another seven days of intravenous antibiotic therapy. This was two months after my surgery.

After Victor dropped me off, he never came back all week. He would call me on my cell phone two times during the week. One nurse left an intravenous needle in my arm and never came back. I had to go out into the hallway and call for a nurse. Unfortunately for me, this time around, none of them spoke English.

The doctor who performed my surgery came into my room and asked me why I was back in the hospital. I told him I did not know because I don't speak the native language fluently. He called for a nurse to change my intravenous needle. I thanked him for saving my life. Then he left.

Another nurse came in and did a bad job taking my intravenous needle out. Blood was squirting out everywhere. She was laughing. I didn't find any humor in this at all. She told me that I had to go down the hallway to see another doctor. I asked why. She told me that I needed an exam. She brought me to a room where a gynecologist wanted to do an internal exam.

Victor came the next day to see when I could go home. He must have run out of money. I had to go to pay the bill for the private room before they would take my IV out.

When I got home, I went to sleep. When I woke up, Victor was gone, and he would not return until the early hours of the morning.

I thought if I could only stay out of the hospital long enough, I could make some plans to end all this insanity once and for all.

On his birthday, there was a wine festival up north near the Romanian border. We got up early that morning and walked about thirty minutes to the northern side of the village to catch the bus that was going up north. We sat at the bus stop and waited for a bus that never came. That was the defining moment of our relationship. We were always waiting for something that would never arrive.

CHAPTER 9

Devalued

After the wine festival disappointment, Victor was never home, but when he was, he would be on his laptop chatting with somebody. After I gave him some money to go get us some food, I quickly became irrelevant immediately afterward.

It was around this time that Victor told me that he wanted to pursue a Hungarian passport so he could get a US visa. Guess who paid for this? Me! He became proficient at extorting money out of me for deceptive reasons.

Sometimes I would walk by his laptop and notice he was using an online translator. I wondered who he might be talking to. The language looked like Russian. After that, he would leave again all day and all night. I would spend this time reading the news on American websites. It helped me to keep my American identity and to know what was going on in the world. It also helped to take my mind off the fact that I was in a rat bastard marriage.

It became clear to me why he never taught me his language and why I never had any interest to learn it on my own. I was finally having some aha moments, and that was a good sign.

Victor thought I didn't want to go anywhere with him while I was recovering from surgery because I didn't love him. I didn't want to go anywhere with Victor because I didn't like him. He was financially abusive and very deceptive.

Victor told me one day that he was going up to Russia to learn the language so he could get some job training and hopefully, a job. I thought, *Great*! At least he was willing to make some type of an attempt to do something with his life that would make him financially independent. Although I found this suspicious since Victor admitted to me on several occasions that he took Russian language in school and hated every minute of it. Guess who paid for his airline ticket? Victor's destination airport was not in Russia. For me, Victor's attempt to contribute was too little too late. His deception was so obvious.

Two days before his departure date arrived, I started bleeding heavy again. On the day he left, his mother took me to the hospital. While I was standing there talking to the nurse, my blood pressure took a fast dive. I told her I felt like I was going to pass out. She went and got me a chair to sit in. After she finished asking questions, she brought me to a hospital bed that was in a room with five other women. She told me to put a pad on so she could see how much blood I was losing and how many pads I was going through. When I took my pants off, my underwear hit the floor with a thud from the weight of the overfull pad I already had on. I told her that I didn't need a pad. I needed a *fucking* bucket! It was running down both of my legs! She never came back to make that assessment either. Another nurse came in to take me down the hall to the gynecologist for an exam. I was then sent back to my bed, where I fell asleep for the night.

When I awoke the next morning, I felt wet. I pulled my blanket off and noticed that my bed and I were covered in blood. I was horrified! There was always a doctor and nurses who came around the same time every morning to assess every patient. When they got to me, I pulled my blankets down, and they could see that my bed and I were covered with a severe amount of blood.

The doctor said to me, "Do not eat anything!"

I said, "Don't worry!" I must have been white as a ghost due to a large amount of blood loss.

Two hours later, after marinating in a pool of my own blood, a nurse came in to clean me up. She then took me to another room where about ten people were standing.

I was instructed to get up on the table and put my feet in the stirrups. An intravenous needle was put into my hand. I turned to the medicine nurse who was holding the button and said to her, "Please knock me the fuck out!" They all laughed, and within seconds, I was under and unaware of what was going on, which was how I preferred all my medical procedures.

I woke up afterward in a clean bed. A nurse came in and told me that I was being discharged. I told her that she had to call my mother-in-law and tell her to come pick me up. Victor's mother was there in about an hour while I was getting ready to leave. I was a bit slow walking. She was miles ahead of me like Victor always was, which I thought was disconcerting.

It was almost the end of November, and I was alone besides his mother and brother's three kids. I decided to make the best of it, so I took out the Christmas tree and decorated it. Despite being alone, I was actually very happy for some reason for the first time in a long time. I bought some wood, brought it into my room after I split it. My method of splitting wood with an ax was to crank I hate you heavy metal music and see Victor's face as the wood. I had a nice tall stack in no time.

Before Victor left, I had bought some new furniture to make our lives and our room nicer. It was getting wicked cold by now, so I had a nice fire in the woodstove to keep me warm.

I started to go out into the village to buy my own stuff. I would use the online translator to find the right words for what I wanted. My language and his never did translate well. I did get a lot of people with no patience concerning my native language skills; nonetheless, I managed to get what I needed by pointing to things that were behind the glass case. The merchants in the village and Victor's family members learned sign language because I was so good at it. They also learned how to read my facial expressions. I was good at that too.

I used Victor's pickled hot peppers to make some spicy Szechuan beef, pork, and chicken with vegetables over rice. I also made some soup with stuffed peppers. I ate good while Victor was away. I also made some chocolate pie for my niece and two nephews.

During this time, one of my nephews would keep asking me for money for various things. I would give him a few bucks here and there. When he started to ask for more money, I had to say no. Apparently, Victor's mother was raising a second generation of men with a grandiose sense of entitlement. The woman had no shame. She preferred to spend other peoples' money and not hers.

Victor's brother also was said to have gone to Russia to work a few weeks before he went. He left his kids with his mother all winter. The kids' mother would come over to spend some time with them.

Every time I went out, Victor tried to contact me on Skype. His mother and the kids would tell me to talk to Victor on Skype. One day, he did send me a Skype call, and we spoke. I asked him some questions about how his endeavor was going, and he would tell me. He told me the name of the company he was training to work for. It was a grocery store. I asked him what job he was pursuing—cashier or counter stalker? He said he was interested in being hired as a web developer. After he said that, I had an aha moment.

I noticed that around a certain time of day, he was available and wanted to communicate with me, but there were other times when he was not available.

I started to get a sense of him communicating with me around another person's schedule. He would tell me that it was dinner time, and he had to go down the hall to eat dinner with the rest of the guys. When he was at his so-called apartment, he was always sitting on a couch with a picture of a naked lady in the background.

Victor sent me some pictures of the building he was staying in. I would find out later that this was a lie. Big surprise! He also sent me a picture of him with some woman, and he said that she was some grandmother who lived down the hall. I thought this was strange considering he was there with other guys trying to learn a language to obtain a job. I saw other pictures of him that were sent by him for me to see what looked like he was having the time of his life; however, when we spoke on Skype, he would paint a picture of discontent.

Something just wasn't right with this picture. Victor's actions never matched his words.

I started asking Victor some trick questions to trip him up, and it worked. I asked him if I could see where he slept. I figured if he was sleeping with some woman, the bed would look like a woman's bed. He said, "Maybe tomorrow." He never showed me. I would find out later why. My intuition was correct on that one. I wish my intuition told me at the beginning of this relationship to run! Sometimes it is fun to be right but not in cases like this.

Victor told me that on Christmas day, he was invited to dinner at that grandmother's apartment, whose son Victor went to class with—another lie. I did not see or hear from him on Christmas Day, New Year's Eve, and New Year's Day. *Not a good way to start out the new year*, I thought, but it was a prelude for things to come.

I would have a few dark nights after this, where I cried myself to sleep because I had all sorts of things going through my mind that were particularly unsettling. I started to feel much better afterward. I was getting stronger by the day. Cutting wood for heat helped tremendously.

It was time for me to remember everything Victor did during our relationship that was harmful to me. The time had come for me to do what I needed to for me. I needed to liberate myself from all this adversity Victor had caused in my life. I was done being used and taken for granted.

I knew that Victor was a liar. I didn't deserve any of it. Despite all this, he used me up for as much as he could get. It was time for me to fully let go of Victor. It was getting a lot easier day by day. I realized that I was not holding onto him anymore. He was letting me go. I decided that it was past due for me to cut the cord!

One day, I walked out of our room and was shocked by what I saw. His mother was covered in blood up to her elbows with blood clots all over. I saw buckets filled with blood, pig meat, and intestines. The room had about five tables with pig flesh on them. I said out loud, "What a lovely room of death!" The smell was so overpowering that I almost vomited.

Before Victor left supposedly for Russia, I asked him if I could use his Facebook page to be able to communicate with friends and family back in the United States. He must have forgotten that he gave me his password because he was so happy having such a wonderful time.

While Victor was gone, my friends and family contacted me to ask if I was still with him. I said, "That's debatable." They told me that they found a Facebook page with him on it passing himself off to be something he was not. It was called "Microsoft." He had another one called "Witches and Pagans." The second one is the one he gave me his password for and the one he had since I met him seven years ago.

I told them to e-mail me some screenshots of everything. They were hesitant because of the nature of the content. "Just sent me the photos!" I said. Victor's secret squirrel Facebook page was identical to the one he had when he was pursuing me. I still have those screenshots of it. It was lies, lies, and more lies about who he was and where he was from. This time, he put he was from Los Angeles, California. The one he gave me seven years ago said he was from Beverly Hills, California. What tangled webs we weave, when first we practice, to deceive. It looks like my description of Victor as being a snake was coming to light. I even had photos to document that he was, in fact, Kaa, the snake with the swirly hypnotic eyes.

I was beginning to see a pattern here. What really caught my eye though was his lie about his employment. He said he used to work at some fictitious company and left to go and work for Microsoft. Microsoft is in Redmond, Washington, and not in Los Angeles, California. I would know this being from the United States. It became apparent to me that I spent a lot of money on his web development and business English, not for us but for him. Victor is cold and calculating, and my life would be so much better without him in it.

It became obvious he might have been involved with someone else since at least 2012. There were pictures on this profile that painted a whole new picture about his life. Victor's "Microsoft" Facebook profile said he was single. Last time I checked, we were still living together and legally married. I would see pictures of what

I concluded were two different women, but later, I could see just one person. She must have been two-faced, like Victor. I was glad he finally met his match—just not at my expense.

I remembered Victor telling me that he had to go cut the grass for some woman in the village who was never home because she was always in another country.

I was told by my friend that I needed to get out of this marriage while I still could. I believe she was fearful for my safety. A family member contacted me on Skype and said that they all knew who she was. They said her profile had my husband all over it. They knew what her name was. I looked her up, and my jaw hit the floor. My sorrow turned to anger. Can someone please tell me why the wife is always the last one to know that her husband is a cad?

The signs were written all over the wall. My intuition was telling me that this was so. I took his tarot deck out and gave myself a reading. Even the cards told me to cut and run—literally! I was drawing cards that indicated some major deception and betrayal.

Victor contacted me on Skype a few days after New Year, wanting to see how I was. Even though I just wanted to smash his face in, I kept my recent discovery to myself, swallowed my pride, and rolled with it.

While we were on Skype, I noticed Victor was silent for a while. I went onto his Facebook page with the Wiccans and Pagans—the one he gave me the password for. He was chatting with some woman.

I thought back to how he had highjacked my Facebook page and said nasty things to people on my friends list, that cost me valuable long-term friendships. I figured it was my turn to give him a taste of his own medicine. I pretended to be him, and I started saying things to her that were demeaning and downright derogatory like he did to my family and friends. At this point, it felt pretty good too. After about five comments, he finally figured out it was me. She signed off. Victor asked me what I thought I was doing, and I told him, "Payback is a bitch for all those ignorant comments you made to my friends and family." I said, "How does it feel?"

Victor told me that her husband was considering being a cosponsor for his US visa. Because of the things I said to her, he lost that chance according to him. I said, "Well, that's what you get for what you did to me."

He said to me, "When I get home, you will be see what you will be get!" Not quite sure what the hell that meant, but I took it as a threat. I told him that it was time for him to come home. I had to go to his travel agent to change the return date on his ticket, and I had to pay for it too.

He was not happy about cutting his good time lie short. I contacted US immigration in the capital of his country and documented his threat. I was told that when a United States citizen travels to another country, there is not much the embassy can do for them. They are considered to have gone at their own risk.

Victor contacted me again on Skype the next day. I just engaged him in small talk. Someone else sent me a friend request on Skype—some woman. She could not speak English and had to use an online translator. I knew who she was from her location and her picture. She said a lot of things to me that she could only have gotten from Victor, like his distorted lies about me and our marriage.

I told her that he does not work at Microsoft. That Microsoft is not even in California. It is in Washington state. I also told her that he was not from California and that he never stepped foot into the United States and would never get the chance to go to the United States, at least not on my dime. I told her that he did not work during our entire six-year marriage. I also told her that he did not work during his first marriage either. I told her that I supported him, and now that I was going to be ending our rat bastard marriage, she should start supporting Victor financially immediately. I was done! I also sent her the bill for how much I spent supporting him during our six-year marriage, including the price of the airline tickets I bought for him to be with her just to give her a picture of how much he was going to cost her and how much of a lying rat Victor really was. She was surprised when she found out that I was living in his country. Everything I told her about him I'm sure corrected many lies he told her. I also thanked her for giving me my life back by being his backdoor girl. I told her she could have him with my full blessing. That pissed him off! I then ended my conversation with this low-life homewrecker who did not even have the balls to show her face on Skype.

There is a special place in hell for women who have affairs with married men although it can be a blessing for the wife to rid herself of such trash. The married men will be joining these lowlifes in hell too.

Then I went back to take a good look at him. He asked me who I was talking to.

"Just your average run of the mill low-life homewrecker," I said with a smile. She was probably sitting right there beside him on that couch with the naked lady picture in the background. Without another word, I pressed the sign-out button.

> Psychological abuse is insidious, and it occurs over time, like an intravenous drip of poison entering your veins.
> —Shannon Thomas LCSW, Author
> of *Healing from Hidden Abuse*

All I could do was split wood, pretending that the wood was his face to release my anger. I had to get unstuck from this toxic cycle.

CHAPTER 10

Double Discard

When I went to go pick Victor up at the airport, the female taxi driver that he knew told me to go inside to greet him. He was not in the area where his arrival was. When I walked back out to the taxi, he came up from behind me. I turned around and went to hug him, and he pushed me away. I concluded that he was not in his arrival area because he was not alone. Whoever he was with left the airport separately. That's the feeling I got. I also thought that he might have never left his country in the first place. Why then would he not be in his flight arrival area? Why would the female taxi driver urge me to go inside to greet him? Why did he walk up to the taxi from outside the airport? Another suspicious event in our lives.

All the way from the airport back home, Victor only spoke his native language to the female taxi driver, not a damn word to me. I was just the money tree. He had her drop us off down the sidewalk about a hundred feet. He didn't want others to know how poor he truly was. That was only for me.

The time had finally come for me to end this marriage.

I had no more sorrow or confusion about anything that involved Victor anymore. My sorrow had turned to justifiable anger.

Victor wanted to know what there was for him to eat. I told him to eat *shit*. He shot me an evil glare. I told him there was slaughtered pig in the freezer compliments of his mother and to help himself. Victor said he was not interested in that. I told him, "Too bad, so sad, that's all you have!"

The next day was my fiftieth birthday. What was supposed to be a celebrated milestone in my life ended up becoming a day filled with sadness and anxiety. I had to look at this in a whole new light. My freedom, and the wisdom I would gain from it.

The day after my birthday, I confronted Victor with pictures of his girlfriend and words he wrote under her picture. He denied it all as he swallowed hard. He looked me right in the eyes with an evil look and lied to me—not the first time, but it would be his last. Victor asked me if he could have some money for food. I told him those days were over. If he needed someone to support him, he could contact his girlfriend and ask her for money to support his *ass*. Victor told me that he did not have a girlfriend. I told him that pictures and words do not lie. He told me that those pictures were all photoshopped. Yeah, not buying it, motherfucker!

Victor took me to go see his brother's girlfriend the next day, you know, the one that destroyed his marriage. I guess cheating on your wife ran in his family genes.

Victor told her to prepare divorce papers for us while the whole time denying his deceit. He did not talk to me. He only spoke to her in their native language, so, of course, I could not understand what they were saying.

When we got to the courthouse, we were told that they were not the properly formatted divorce documents. I asked him flat out, "Did you cheat on me?"

He again looked me in the eyes and said no, but I could tell by the blank stare on his face that he was lying. He was never that good at lying anyway.

That day, apparently, Victor's girlfriend thought our divorce was filed. On her Facebook page, she posted a picture of the two of them kissing each other inside of a heart. He told me again that all these photos of the two of them were photoshopped. Yeah, not buying it!

The next day, I went to meet with a divorce lawyer that was recommended to me by the US embassy. I gave my lawyer pictures of my husband with his girlfriend, a screenshot of his Microsoft

Facebook page where he claimed to be single, and copies of his flight schedule from the plane tickets.

Victor was not supposed to have left his country if, in fact, he did. I wonder if he never left his country and got a refund on the tickets. The reason why is because according to immigration in his country, he was responsible for my safety, or was that just his excuse to isolate me by thinking that I was dependent on him?

I paid my foreign divorce lawyer to file the necessary documents with the court to end this marriage as soon as possible.

The second time I saw my lawyer, he told me that I could leave the country before the final divorce hearing by hiring a power of attorney, which I gladly did. I paid him cash right there on the spot. He also told me that I needed to hire an English translator for a meeting with the power of attorney. The next time I had to go speak to my lawyer, Victor insisted on coming with me. I didn't want him around me, I was having anxiety attacks. I couldn't breathe because I wanted to smash his face in. My lawyer witnessed my anxiety and said to me, "Are you all right?" I didn't answer him.

Victor and my lawyer spoke in front of me in their native language for about fifteen minutes. I started to space off to a happier time in my life.

Suddenly, my lawyer yelled, "Lady, do you understand me?"

I said, "No, I don't, so if you could just put all of the papers together for us to sign, that would be wonderful."

My lawyer told us to meet him in one hour at an address he gave Victor. When we arrived at the power of attorney's office, Victor tried to kiss me outside when we got there. What a jerk! I pushed him away then walked into the building and went up the stairs to another episode of the twilight zone.

The so-called English translator read me what I needed to know concerning my divorce in English. I mean, it was really written in English. I could have read the damn thing by myself. What an *asshole*! I paid her fee, and I told her that she was a good con artist, just like my soon-to-be ex-husband. Nonetheless, progress was rolling toward my freedom, and that's all I cared about. The cost was of no concern to me. I was just so sick and tired of being lied to and shafted by these people.

Victor and I had eight weeks of in-your-face moments, and I embraced every *motherfucking* single one! He said to me, "After you leave, I never want to see or hear from you again!"

I said, "Don't worry, you won't!"

I arranged on purpose for Victor and I to sign our divorce papers in front of my lawyer on Valentine's Day. Then we went to the courthouse to file the documentation to start the divorce process. I wanted to mock him by doing this on Valentine's Day since our marriage was a sham on his part all along.

On our way back to the bus station, I stopped in front of a florist. Victor said, "What are you doing?"

I looked Victor straight in the eyes, smiled, and said to him, "Today is Valentine's Day, and I have never been more in love with myself than I am at this very moment!" All the blood ran from his face until he was ghostly white. "What's the matter, Victor?" I said. "Did you forget your new sweetie on the international day of love?" Of course, how can a cad know when Valentine's Day is?

I walked into the flower shop, bought myself one single red rose, a bottle of white zinfandel and some Lindor chocolates. Victor followed me into the shop, and I told him out loud that he should wait outside because there wasn't enough space inside for him. I was embracing every in-your-face moment. While we were sitting at the bus stop waiting for the bus to come, I said, "Hey, why don't you send your girlfriend a Valentine's Day graphic on Facebook since that's all you can manage?" I knew that he extorted money out of me to make his girlfriend think that he had money. Victor more than likely bought her gifts for the holidays with money that he previously stole from me under false pretenses. What a cad! I sat there and sniffed my rose while waiting for the bus.

Victor said as he shot me an evil glare, "I don't have a girlfriend."

I said out loud, "Girlfriend, mistress, whore, prostitute, whatever she is, I spoke to her on Skype, and she confirmed your whole relationship, so you can't deny her. I also saw her Facebook profile with you all over it. She has a face and a name."

He just looked at me in anger. Victor's face turned beet red from embarrassment. There was a handful of people standing there from his village, also waiting for the bus. He knew that no matter how much he denied her, the more it was obvious that she couldn't be denied. He was caught with his pants down, and this time, I was not going to look at him. All the way back to the village, his face was still red with anger.

When we returned to his home, I turned on my laptop computer with stereo speakers and put on some music. Victor started to shoot me some dirty looks. To piss him off extra, I played his tribute song to me from our wedding—the Bryan Adams song, "Everything I do, I do it for You!" I told him that the irony of that song was that he never did *shit* for me; he was just taking care of himself all this time at my expense.

I continued to sniff my rose, drink my wine, and eat my chocolates right in front of him. Now that I had Victor's full attention, I played "More than Words" from Extreme full blast while holding up my middle finger.

Victor asked if he could have some chocolate. I said, "No, but you can contact your girlfriend and ask her to send you some."

"I don't have a girlfriend!" he said. He then asked me what we were going to be eating.

"There is no we," I said. "Go feed your own ego. I'm busy." I said. Then I played Godsmack's "Whatever!"

Victor stood up and left for the rest of the day and night. Good! I didn't enjoy his company anyway. I listened to some more good breakup music and had chocolate and wine for the day and passed out. He came home late. I did ask him to leave, but he said he had nowhere to go. I suggested that he go to hell! Can you imagine how difficult it is to have to sleep next to somebody you hate? I just wanted to smash his face in!

Victor said to me the next day that he was going to sue me because he could not get a US visa. I said, "Good. Please do it so I can have your US immigration marriage fraud documented." Then I informed him that US immigration marriage fraud carried a $250,000 fine plus the potential to serve a prison term of up to five years. He shut his pie hole after that. I asked Victor if his girlfriend put him up to that. He sat there and gave me a dirty look. I asked him how much money did he extort from me and give to her. He walked out of the room in a huff.

Victor told me how his friends and family were criticizing me for my words and actions. I laughed and told him, "Of course, they are on your side, numbnuts." I informed him that nobody in my camp was on his side either, especially the ones that sent me the pictures of him with another woman. He proceeded to tell me that my family were nothing but a bunch of criminals. Give me a break! Besides, what did my family have to do with his behavior? Not a damn thing.

Every time Victor said something stupid to me, I quickly shot him down until he no longer had a leg to stand on. There was no argument he could win with me. I was ten steps ahead of his every evil word.

During his denial of his indiscretions, he persisted to ask me for all kinds of *shit*. "What part of you fucked up now it's over? Do you not understand?"

If my intuition was correct from the things that Victor's girl-friend said to me, he must have been with her throughout our entire marriage. That would explain why he went from charming to alarming to harming year after year after our wedding.

Maybe he hooked up with her during the eight months while I was in the United States having and recovering from a stroke. I guess our marriage vows translated to English said, "Thou must drain thy wife of her income while lying through thy teeth."

In his twisted mind, he wanted me to feel the way I made him feel when I left him two times to return to the United States. The only difference was that I wasn't replacing him, but he was replacing me. He was doing me a favor without even realizing it.

While Victor was away in another country making future plans for himself, I found many copies of my personal documents way up high, along with three bottles of plum brandy. I drank two bottles and left him one, the one I could not reach, and he was pissed.

I told Victor that if he tries to pass his new girlfriend off as me, it will never work because she does not have my fingerprints, and she really does not look identical to me. When she is caught immediately for identity fraud/theft, she will be taken from the airport and put into federal prison for many years. I told him to go for it! He just might try to pull that one off just to unload her too when he has no more use for her as well. Hopefully, US Customs will see him as an accomplice and arrest him too. One can only hope!

According to the photographs I have seen of the two of them, Victor started putting his last name on her name, like he did with me in the beginning. With each passing day, I was more and more relieved that his con-man sham was finally coming to an end. His life was finally blowing up in his face. I was free!

I had a few last-minute loose ends to tie up. I had to contact my doctor in the village. I went to go see her about getting a letter so I could travel to the United States with European pharmaceuticals. I also showed her my impending divorce papers. She gave me her e-mail if I needed anything else. I showed her the pictures of Victor and his girlfriend. She told me that she knew all about Victor and his family and that she did not blame me for ending the relationship. She wished me well and told me to keep in touch.

It was only a matter of time before my departure date arrived, which would have been our sixth wedding anniversary. I figured since our marriage meant nothing to Victor but a US visa and a green card, then the only thing our anniversary meant to me was my freedom. Filing our divorce papers on Valentine's Day and leaving him on our sixth wedding anniversary was my final *fuck* you!

When my departure date finally arrived. It was time for me to get ready. I put all my stuff near the door and waited till the ride he arranged was ready.

Victor said to me that I was old and that nobody would want me. I said to him, "What makes you think that I need anybody? And why would I care at this point what you think anyways?"

He started talking *shit* to me about how I could file a fiancé visa for him once I returned to the United States. I thought to myself, *Wow what a nerve!* I just went along with everything he said because, at this point, he was behaving frantically because now he would have to go out and work for once in his life instead of using another person for his own gain. I could not believe that he really thought that I would go along with anything he had to say. His time had run out.

I said, "Yeah, right, sure, fiancé visa." I would have said anything to get the *fuck* out of the twilight zone for good for the last time. Alive! He was becoming unhinged. When it came time for me to walk out the door for the last time, his mother was standing outside our door crying. I hugged her and the three kids that I watched grow up for the past seven years. Then I left for the airport. It was a quiet ride aside from me humoring him with anything he had to say. When we arrived at the airport, he put my two suitcases up on the counter and made a comment about the four Muslims who were waiting in line fighting, and with that, he was gone. Cao, babe! Good riddance to bad luck!

The four Muslim passengers on that flight to London sat three rows in front of me—three in front of me and one on the other side of the plane. They kept lighting cigarettes up one after another. Every time they did, the flight attendant came to have a serious conversation with them.

The British passengers on the plane started to have a verbal fight with the four Muslims. One Muslim stood up and walked up to the cockpit then back to his seat. I sat there looking out my window seat just thinking to myself, *I just want to live!*

My opinion of those four Muslims, is that they had no respect for us or our laws. To make a long story short, they were detained by British Airways security and taken off the plane by the London police upon arrival. That incident, by the way, never made it into the news. At least I have never been able to find it.

Because of that incident on that flight, I barely made it to my connecting flight. Flying over the Atlantic one more time was bittersweet for me. When I arrived at my port of entry airport, I noticed a whole different system put into place by US Customs. I missed the first bus, and I had to wait for the next one.

Once I was finally on the next bus an hour later and heading north, I took out my laptop to check my e-mail. There was a message on my computer that said my version of MS Windows 2007 was not genuine. I laughed out loud. Apparently, neither was my marriage. For all the times he took my laptop to be fixed, along with the money to pay for it, he gave me back a counterfeit version. I spent seven years in a counterfeit relationship.

Although I did love Victor in the beginning, our marriage never should have taken place. It was just so wrong. We didn't have anything in common. We were from two different worlds. I didn't fit into his world, and I doubt that he ever would have fit into mine.

I looked out my window into the nighttime city lights with a big smile on my face. I was finally free or pretty damn close to it. I was done being involved with a cad for seven years in the twilight zone!

It is our worst experiences in life that eventually make us who we become. If it doesn't kill you, it will only make you stronger. A better version of yourself will rise from the ashes like a phoenix.

CHAPTER 11

A Means to an End

Unfortunately for me, it didn't end there. After I left Victor's country and returned to the United States, he continued to send me harassing e-mails.

Victor threatened to stop the divorce. According to Victor, he was told by his family that if we divorced, he would lose his chances of ever getting a US visa. I told him that as of our final divorce hearing in two weeks, that would make us family no more.

How can you divorce someone anyway if they married you under fraudulent pretenses? I always wondered if my foreign marriage was even legal. My previous divorce gave me a name change. Victor's country used the name on my passport, which was different from my legal name at the time.

Again, Victor threatened to cancel our divorce the following Monday morning. I told him that I would cancel my family visa petition with US immigration and that would end his visa application. He told me that I had six days to cancel our divorce. I told him that I looked forward to not being married to him anymore. He demanded that I see and talk with him on Skype. I told him to take a hike! Those days were over. He then demanded that I contact him on WhatsApp. I told him that I don't have that. He told me then to keep his name. I told him that I was not interested in keeping his name and that he did not deserve any of my time or attention. He also had no right to make any demands of me either.

I wrote the US embassy a letter and attached a copy of my divorce document to it. Two months later, I received a letter from the US embassy in Italy along with the signature of someone at USCIS from the United States that clearly stated that my family visa petition had been withdrawn with no chance of reversing this action. I am pretty sure Victor got a letter also that because of my actions, his visa application was permanently canceled.

Victor must have taken the liberty while he was in front of the foreign judge to misrepresent himself about something so that I would have to keep his last name. I had to file a petition in the United States to go to probate court and change my last name. According to the DMV, in my home state, my translated to English foreign divorce document that I had to pay a New York woman from Victor's homeland did not indicate a legal name change. The US probate judge granted a waiver of all my filing fees and gave me my maiden name back. She probably figured that I got screwed in the foreign divorce and that when I was born, I did not have to pay for my name, so why should I now? That was a good day!

Victor, after being defeated over his US visa, finally came out and confirmed what I knew all along. His lying was over, and he now started sending me pictures of him and his girlfriend. Victor told me that she would not marry him until he divorced me.

Victor continued to send me e-mails. The only one that bothered me was the one where he told me that he was working. He did not work the whole time during our marriage, but he was working now. *What a jerk*, I thought. Good riddance!

Can you imagine what the scenario would have been if Victor did obtain his visa then his green card? He would have divorced me, then he would have been entitled to financial support from me under the I-864 immigration form that I would have signed then sponsored his girlfriend for a K-1 fiancé visa. I am so blessed and thankful that his nefarious plans never came to fruition! I may have suffered for years, but you know what? In the end, I beat him at this own game!

CHAPTER 12

The Hoover

I did not hear from Victor for about a year. What a wonderful year it was too. I could finally breathe again because he was no longer a part of my life. He became someone else's misfortune.

One day, a friend of mine sent me a screenshot of a Facebook page with Victor on it looking smug and still wearing the same clothes I bought him five years ago. The woman on it had such a look on her face that I knew all too well. She looked like she wanted to smash his face in. That's karma! What goes around comes around.

Not too long after that, Victor came out of the blue and decided he was going to send me an e-mail, wishing me a Merry Christmas, happy New Year, and a happy birthday. Those were the very same events in my life that he tried to destroy.

Victor told me that he was working in Holland at an ice cream factory and that we should be in touch. I told him to wish in one hand, *shit* in the other, and see which one fills up faster.

I sent him a music video from Ugly Kid Joe "Everything About You!" In that video, the band is dancing around all over the beach and singing about how happy they are to have unloaded a toxic relationship. *Perfect*, I thought!

Victor told me to forget everything that happened between us. He was putting on some of that old Kaa and Mowgli snake charm of his to appease his guilt. Only the swirly eyes didn't work this time.

I wasn't interested in chewing up any of his old baloney and seeing how it went down.

Victor was hoovering me. It's a term that is used to describe the actions of a classical narcissist trying to *suck* you back into the relationship like a hoover vacuum cleaner. It has nothing to do with love. A narcissist does not love you. They only love themselves. They only use people to get what they want and need because they don't have the ability to achieve anything in life on their own.

I was Victor's supply. I supported him financially. When I left him, he lost his main source of supply. When he went with his girlfriend, she became his new supply. I made a mistake though. You are not supposed to reply to a hoover.

When I sent him that music video, he probably got off on it. He must have been so pleased with himself to know that he had such an effect on me because I hated him so much.

When you end a toxic relationship with a narcissist, it is recommended that you go and stay no contact. Always remember that you're free because you cut the cord and walked away. You no longer need to deal with such a dizzying amount of *bullshit* because you don't deserve it.

In closing, I fell into this twilight zone Third World life because I fell in love, I was being conned, controlled, and manipulated by my ex-foreign national spouse. His megalomania knew no bounds. I always maintained that throughout our seven-year relationship that his actions never matched his words. Individuals with narcissistic and sociopathic characteristics will give you a crash course on how to recognize the truth when words and actions don't match. All you have to do is listen and pay attention. To be able to spot these fun-loving heat seekers from a mile away is priceless!

Resources

Anderson, Donna. *Seduced by a Sociopath: How Antisocials, Narcissists and Psychopaths Use Human Nature Against You.* Anderly Publishing (November 15, 2019).

Moore, Thomas. *Dark Nights of the Soul: A Guide to Finding Your Way Through Life's Ordeals.* Penguin Random House (June 16, 2005).

Smith, Jennifer. *Breaking Up with Evil: Escaping Coercive Control.* Blogger Industries (February 14, 2020).

Thomas, Shannon. *Healing from Hidden Abuse: A Journey Through the Stages of Recovery from Psychological Abuse.* MAST Publishing House (August 25, 2016).

Immigrationfraud.com

uscis.gov

truelovescam.com

lovefraud.com

darleneanolin.com

About the Author

Darlene Ann Nolin was born in Nashua, and raised in Pelham, New Hampshire. She lived in Europe for six years. She currently resides in Waterville, Maine. She has three adult kids, and five grandchildren. In addition to working for many years in government and private-sector jobs in the capacity of an administrative assistant, she has also fulfilled her dreams of becoming an author. She attended Southern New Hampshire University, where she studied English and creative writing. When she is not writing or posting on her blog: https://darleneanolin.com she enjoys spending time with her grandchildren, spending the day at the Atlantic Ocean, kayaking in Flanders bay, traveling, camping, drawing, Tai Chi, Yoga, Pilates, exercising, cooking, and maintaining an active, healthy lifestyle. She is also an avid reader and book reviewer.